Praise for
Shaken

"Tim Tebow is not an athlete—*athlete* is what Tim fills in on his tax return. That does not begin to tell the story of who he is. Tim is a role model, an inspiration to those who have a dream and are willing to accept life as a journey full of ups and downs."

—JON BON JOVI, singer-songwriter

"*Shaken* shows us a side of Tim Tebow that we've never gotten to see before. In this book, Tim comes alongside his reader and says, 'I've been there too,' and proceeds to show us how God is faithful even when our entire lives feel shaken to the core."

—MARK BATTERSON, pastor and *New York Times* best-selling
author of *The Circle Maker*

"Tim is a remarkable example of one who combines strength and boldness with kindness and compassion, and I'm always encouraged to hear of how he is using his tremendous platform to share the love and truth of our Lord with those who need it most."

—RAVI ZACHARIAS, apologist, author, and president of RZIM

"Tim has always inspired me with his dedication to grow and improve in all aspects of life, especially his faith. With this book, Tim encourages readers to keep moving and stay strong while battling life's obstacles."

—CAM NEWTON, quarterback for the Carolina Panthers

"Whether or not you've followed Tim's career, *Shaken* speaks to something we've all had to deal with—trusting God when the plans for our lives don't work out as we expected. Tim shares his journey from the Broncos to the Jets to the Patriots and beyond with refreshing honesty. He comes alongside us as a friend and gives us hope for the days our lives take an unexpected turn. I am so grateful to call Tim my friend; his life and passion constantly inspire me! Whatever Tim does he does with all his heart, and this book reflects that incredible commitment! I love Tim, and by the end of this book, you will too!"

—JUDAH SMITH, lead pastor of the City Church and *New York Times* best-selling author of *Jesus Is* _____.

"*Shaken* is everyone's story. All of us know what it is to experience the best of days and the lowest of days. For Tim, he's lived those days in public. I have the privilege to call Tim my friend and can tell you that with him, what you see is what you get, which seems rare these days! I appreciate how real and raw Tim is with his own struggles. In *Shaken* you will find great encouragement for your own life and faith."

—CHRIS TOMLIN, worship leader and songwriter

TIM TEBOW

WITH A. J. GREGORY

NEW YORK TIMES BESTSELLER

SHAKEN

DISCOVERING YOUR TRUE IDENTITY
IN THE MIDST OF LIFE'S STORMS

WATERBROOK

Trade Paperback ISBN 978-0-7352-8988-8
Hardcover ISBN 978-0-7352-8986-4
eBook ISBN 978-0-7352-8987-1

Text copyright © 2016 by Timothy R. Tebow
Introduction copyright © 2018 by Timothy R. Tebow

Cover design by Kristopher Orr; cover photograph by Bryan Soderlind

Published in the United States by WaterBrook, an imprint of the Crown Publishing Group, a division of Penguin Random House LLC, New York.

WATERBROOK® and its deer colophon are registered trademarks of Penguin Random House LLC.

The Library of Congress has cataloged the hardcover edition as follows:
Names: Tebow, Tim, 1987– author.
Title: Shaken / Tim Tebow, with AJ Gregory.
Description: First Edition. | Colorado Springs, Colorado : WaterBrook, 2016. | Includes bibliographical
    references.
Identifiers: LCCN 2016029470 (print) | LCCN 2016033006 (ebook) | ISBN 9780735289864 (hard cover) |
    ISBN 9780735289871 (electronic)
Subjects: LCSH: Identity (Psychology)—Religious aspects—Christianity. | Success—Religious
    aspects—Christianity.
Classification: LCC BV4509.5 .T43 2016 (print) | LCC BV4509.5 (ebook) | DDC 248.4—dc23
LC record available at https://lccn.loc.gov/2016029470

Printed in the United States of America
2018—First Trade Paperback Edition

10 9 8 7 6 5 4 3 2 1

SPECIAL SALES
Most WaterBrook books are available at special quantity discounts when purchased in bulk by corporations, organizations, and special-interest groups. Custom imprinting or excerpting can also be done to fit special needs. For information, please e-mail specialmarketscms@penguinrandomhouse.com or call 1-800-603-7051.

To the two best things in my life:

Jesus, the greatest gift I ever received.

My family. The thing about family is that you don't get to pick them. But if I could, I'd choose every one of you. I love you, Mom, Dad, Christy, Katie, Robby, and Peter!

Contents

INTRODUCTION

One thing can change everything. A win. A loss. A smart decision. A bad review. A season of success. A season of failure. The color of your skin. According to the world, at least, it seems that one thing can determine who you are—or make you question it.

Over the course of my public life, the world has tried to force me onto a roller coaster of identities—defining me by my circumstances and not by who I really am. Was my identity found in the highs when I won the Heisman Trophy and later when the Denver Broncos were making a play-off run? No. Was my identity found when, a year later, I was cut? No.

One day, as headlines told it, I was at the top of my game—adored, praised, and respected. And the next, I was at the bottom of the heap—cut, criticized, and torn down. You know what I've learned in the process? How important it is not to allow either the highs or the lows in life dictate who you are.

It's tempting to define ourselves or measure our worth by the external: by how much money we have, by how we look, by the applause of others. The list is long. It's also tempting to determine our identity by our life circumstances. Think about this: Who are you when everything is going great—when the money is in the bank, when your marriage is picture perfect, when your future seems certain? And who are you when your world is shaken—when you're barely making it paycheck to paycheck, when your relationship is on the fritz, when you haven't a clue what tomorrow holds? Sometimes it takes a challenging time to really find out.

While many know about my career highs, few know the details about the lows. Like having to learn that God's plans are better and bigger than mine, feeling torn about the future, and working through one of my dreams being shattered after getting cut from three NFL teams. I admit that writing this book hasn't been easy. It was tough to relive some painful moments. But I'll say it was in those places of doubt and even of darkness that I've realized that who I am has nothing to do with wins or losses, applause or negative criticism.

My identity is tied into *whose* I am. Knowing this, I can live out what the king of ancient Israel wrote in Psalm 16:8:

I have set the LORD continually before me;
Because He is at my right hand, I will not be shaken.

Although in this book I share parts of my personal life and football journey in the NFL, this is not a memoir. It's about the truth I've discovered along the way. And it's about some amazing people who have inspired me in life as well as through our foundation's W15H (pronounced "wish") outreach program. Though our mission is to bring faith, hope, and love to those needing a brighter day in their darkest hour of need, without fail, they have given those very things to me. While I wish I could tell you about every single child and family I've met who've inspired me, I'm excited to be able to share a few stories with you.

Here's what you can expect to find in this book. The first seven chapters will reveal some of the lows I've experienced, glimpses into my life, and parts of myself that I've never shared publicly. They'll also uncover the lessons I've learned through that time, like what it means to stay grounded in the face of doubt, fear, and criticism; why others matter; and how our objective in life is not to be like everyone else.

The final three chapters focus on how we can impact others. When we are grounded in whose we are, not only can we handle the storms that come, but we can also begin to move forward in a more purposeful direction. We can begin to live in a new way. We can influence the lives of others even when our circumstances look bleak. We can use our stories to help others in their own.

Since the release of the hardcover edition of *Shaken,* some exciting things have happened. I decided to pursue one of my passions since childhood—baseball. At the time of this writing, I'm playing pro ball with the New York Mets. It's been a wild ride, filled with—yup, you guessed it—highs and lows. During this journey I've had to remind myself of many of the truths I share in this book. I don't know how this path will pan out, but I'm certain of one thing: God's got this!

Another thing I'm psyched about is how much Night to Shine has grown since it began in 2015. Our foundation partners with churches around the world to host proms for guests with special needs. It's my favorite night of the year! In 2017, God took the Night to Shine movement, in just its third year, to 375 churches in the United States and eleven foreign countries. Amazing volunteers all over the world gave seventy-five thousand honored guests a night they'll never forget. Not only that, but we served more than one thousand guests in my hometown of Jacksonville, Florida, alone. That's pretty special! I also had the opportunity to honor one of our guests, Judy Adams, on *The Tonight Show Starring Jimmy Fallon.* I can't wait to see where God takes Night to Shine next year. We already have almost five hundred churches signed up!

I'm so thankful I serve a big God. Look, I'm not perfect. I'm on a faith journey just like you are. Sometimes I get it right. Other days I struggle. But I know that when I'm settled in my identity, I live at my best.

I want you to live at your best too.

While this book doesn't offer cookie-cutter answers or a concrete plan about what to do when you stand on shaky ground, it does offer you truth. One thing *can* change everything: knowing who you are in God can give you purpose and reshape your destiny in incredible ways.

When you know this, you will find hope. Your faith will be strengthened. Light will shine on your dark places. You will appreciate how uniquely God made you. And you can even help someone along the way.

This is your time.

Arm yourself with courage and get ready to tackle life and make a difference.

1

CUT

**We must accept finite disappointment,
but we must never lose infinite hope.**

—MARTIN LUTHER KING JR.

The locker room was somber. A strange mixture of sadness, tension, loss. Guys stood in front of giant wooden lockers, where stored on hooks and shoved in corners were more than just sweaty shorts and worn helmets. More than stuff. My teammates were staring at the tangible signs of unmet expectations. Shattered plans. Good old disappointment.

It was late August, time for roster cuts. NFL teams start out with ninety guys, and by the end of the week, the number drops down to fifty-three. And during those seven days, you can't help but feel on edge. Especially as you walk into the locker room after a workout and, from the corner of your eye, see a buddy, someone you trained and worked so hard with, now glum, black trash bags in hand. It was like that all day.

One by one, a handful of my New England Patriots teammates started cleaning out their lockers. Told to go home. That it was over. Some could hide well the obvious disappointment they felt. And with others, it was written all over their faces.

I felt an uncomfortable blend of emotions. On one hand, it wasn't me getting called into a conference room and then later dumping protein shakes, deodorant, and cleats into a noisy trash bag. On the other hand, I felt for them. These were my friends. And their run with the team was done.

As awkwardness hung in the air, weaving through tense, quiet chatter, I clapped one guy on the shoulder and said, "Hey, man. God's got a plan. He's got this." To another, I gave a bear hug, saying nothing.

As the day unfolded, I thought about my standing on the team. I felt like I had gotten more comfortable with my performance. We had just beaten the New York Giants 28–20 the night before, August 29, 2013. In this preseason finale I had finished 6 of 11 in passing for 91 yards with two touchdowns. Yeah, maybe I didn't do my best, but I was just starting to click with the team.

And then, sucker punch.

It was my turn.

———

I didn't see it coming. Maybe because I was one of the last players to get released.

I spent that Friday training in the Patriots facilities at Gillette Stadium. As I worked out, in between squats and deadlifts, I was tuned in to the grim atmosphere. I was probably subconsciously waiting for someone looking for me to pop his head into that room packed with an arsenal of steel exercise equipment. But no one came. That helped to take some of the pressure off, letting me breathe just a little bit easier.

After my workout, it was hard walking into the locker room, where a trail of trash bags and worn football equipment flooded the floor. Seeing teammate after teammate getting released made me tense up again. I said goodbye to the guys while metaphorically looking over my shoulder, waiting for something to happen. Maybe someone to call me into an office. Maybe a text. But nothing. A part of me began to think I was safe, and a sense of security began to sink in.

Sometime earlier, Robert Kraft, the owner of the Patriots and a man I respect and really like, had told me he was looking forward to seeing me at his get-together the next day. He was hosting a barbeque for the team and the staff at his home. Thinking about his words, I felt like it was a sign, a good sign.

Feeling semi-settled, I left the facilities and hung out with my brother Robby and my longtime friends Bryan and Erik. I love these guys. We can be pretty sarcastic with one another and quick with our jabs, but we're also not stingy about offering encouragement when needed. It's a good combo.

Aware of the ongoing cuts and my corresponding tension, my three buddies hung out with me the rest of the day. We hit up a movie theater close to the stadium, hoping a good action flick would help ease some of the remaining tension. And after wasting an hour and a half of our lives watching what was a terribly boring movie, Erik and Bryan headed to the airport to fly home to Jacksonville as Robby and I headed back to the hotel room. As the rest of evening wore on, I still hadn't heard from Coach Bill Belichick or his staff. While the absence of communication boosted my comfort level, I still felt pretty overstrung.

By the time my alarm blared early Saturday morning, I was thinking, *Phew! I made it!* And it was likely in that same breath of relief that I noticed an incoming text message on my phone from Coach.

"Timmy, will you please come in?"

My stomach dropped. I stared at those six words for a minute, my mind reeling. The feeling of security began to shatter.

I drove to the facilities, trying to stay above the mental fray. In moments like these, there's such a temptation to get caught up in the unknown, trying to figure out a situation that's beyond your control. Whatever was going to happen was going to happen. It was that simple. And as equally hard to let sink in.

I tried to focus as I pushed open the glass front doors. The place was practically empty because most of the team was headed to or already at Mr. Kraft's barbeque, which I still had planned to attend. I kept calm as I walked down the gray hallway, not thinking much, my flip-flops flapping noisily on the tiled floor. But when Coach Belichick's poker-faced assistant led me to the sparse conference room, I knew. In an instant.

Enter the sucker punch.

The room was empty, save for a dark wooden rectangular table and a few chairs. There may have been a window or even a tap-dancing flamingo wearing a cocktail dress, but I wouldn't have noticed. My eyes were laser focused on the two men who I was certain were going to change my future on the team.

Coach Belichick sat in a chair on the opposite side of the table. Coach Josh McDaniels, who had drafted me to the Denver Broncos three and a half years earlier, stood in a nearby corner to the left of him. Someone motioned me to sit. Their faces were matter-of-fact, flat, void of expression.

While I can't remember who spoke first or what he said, I think Coach Belichick broke the silence by saying, "Good job on the last game, Timmy."

I nodded, staying quiet. My relationship with Coach Belichick had been good since my Gator days. He would watch me train, encourage me. I liked the guy. And I wanted to play for him, work hard, and prove I was the right choice.

I remembered when I had signed with the team in June. Then I'd had an offer on the table to make a one-day appearance endorsing a product for a million-dollar paycheck. I'm sure you'd agree that a million bucks is a lot to make in just twenty-four hours. But I wasn't quick to say yes.

When I came on the team, Coach and I had a long and deep talk. "I want to make you one of the guys," he told me. "This is not going to be a media circus. I'll control it if you do your part. You're part of a team, Timmy. We're in this together."

So when the offer for the one-day commercial turned up, I was sure to discuss the opportunity with him. "I want to know what you think, Coach," I said. "I respect you and I want to fit in. I want to be one of the guys. Should I do it?"

He thought for a moment and then shook his head. "Timmy, I would really appreciate it if you didn't."

Highly respecting the man, I turned down the deal. I didn't even think twice about it. I wanted the chance to impress Coach Belichick more than I wanted the money. I'll say that if I were on any other team, I would have probably said yes to the offer. But the thoughts he offered in our initial conversation mattered to me—even more than a million dollars.

Back to the conference room.

"It's not the right fit," Coach Belichick said.

My stomach reeled in that moment. I felt disappointed. I felt I had let myself down. I didn't believe I performed as well in practice or the preseason as I could have, but I was getting better. I had been stoked about the opportunity to learn and train under Tom Brady, one of the best quarterbacks of all time, and planned on using that experience to become one of the best quarterbacks of all time too. At the beginning of training camp, I put a lot of pressure on myself to be like Tom and train like Tom and do like Tom, but then I realized it wasn't about being Tom Brady; it was about being me and doing my best. Yet, despite improving my performance during the preseason, my effort wasn't enough.

Frankly, it hurt. I had hoped Coaches Belichick and McDaniels would give me the benefit of the doubt. They were some of my biggest supporters. If they didn't believe in me, who would?

The meeting lasted ten, maybe fifteen minutes. I listened, fixed in posture, not having the courage to take my eyes off these two men. Though I felt they were sincere and genuinely apologetic about the end result, their explanations were vague. I wanted to know what I didn't do or what I should have done, but I didn't get any clarity. Or closure. Just a lot of talking without any answers. I figured my agent would probably call me in a few days and give me a clearer picture.

As Coach Belichick continued to talk, using what I felt were blanket statements, my mind was bombarded by a number of overwhelming thoughts.

Why wasn't I enough? Should I have trained differently? Should I have spent more time studying? Or more time throwing? Is this it?

This wasn't unfamiliar territory for me. In the spring of 2012, I was traded from the Broncos to the New York Jets, a move that felt like a betrayal of sorts. A year later, the Jets let me go. This was a pattern I did not like.

As I nodded, still unwavering in my eye contact, I shifted my thoughts toward God, the One I believed had led me to New England. *I thought this was going somewhere special! I thought this was a plan You designed for me. If that was true, then why, God, why is this thing crashing and burning?*

I thought of the endorsement deal I had turned down two months earlier, questioning and maybe even regretting my decision. *Was it the wrong choice? If I had said yes, would that have put me in a better situation than where I am right now—sitting in front of two coaches who are firing me without telling me exactly why?*

Then, the meeting was over.

I gave Coach Belichick and Coach McDaniels hugs, wishing them and their families well. I genuinely meant what I said. I deeply respected these two men. They are great at what they do. And I didn't blame them in the least. I blamed myself.

As I closed the door behind me, stepping out into the empty hallway that would lead me for the last time to the Patriots locker room and my very own black garbage bags, my heart sank. I felt cornered by regret and its companion, shame. *You could have, you should have done more, Timmy. Why didn't you push harder? Train better? Work out longer?*

I pictured the thousands of letters, cards, and e-mails I had received from kids who looked up to me and had rooted for me. I had failed them. Again.

Thankfully, the locker room was nearly empty, quiet. As I grabbed a few garbage bags and stood in front of my locker, I felt like I was going to throw up. *Is this it? Will I ever wear an NFL uniform again?*

I stared at the bottles and jars of nutritional supplements that cluttered a shelf. Green fuel, protein shakes, vitamins, antioxidants—all the things that were supposed to help me get stronger, faster, better. *Dang,* I thought, *they were no help at all.*

I stared point-blank at the Patriots gear. It taunted me. A uniform I was proud to wear, that I'd never put on again. In a blur, I grabbed some of my personal stuff and chucked the items one by one into a trash bag. As I tossed in a pair of running shoes, I knew the news of my release would be broadcast shortly to millions of Americans.

In the spirit of transparency, I'll say I was embarrassed. I struggled to humble myself and not wallow in the cesspool of conflicting and raw emotions. I knew I'd have to make a statement soon and wanted to do it right. I wanted to say, with total sincerity, that I was grateful to God and to the Patriots for the opportunity.

In that moment, it wasn't easy. I knew God hadn't left me. I knew He still had a plan for my life. I knew He still had a purpose. And though my foundation in Him was solid, much of what rested on top of that was shaken. I love what Mike Tyson reportedly said, something like "Everyone's got a plan until they get punched in the face." That's just what it felt like for me.

A few teammates and coaches were there to say good-bye. They were extremely cordial and supportive, wishing me the best of luck. I can't tell you how much time had passed, but by the time I started filling my second garbage bag, I was over it. I took what I could, left the Patriots equipment untouched, and walked out of the facility, giving more hugs and saying thank-yous to the few people I passed on the way.

The summer sun felt warm on my face, the air calm and still. Walking toward my rental SUV in the middle of a lifeless parking lot, I remembered the last game I had played for the Broncos. On January 14, 2012, the Patriots killed us 45–10 in the second round of the AFC Championship play-offs. During the game, unknown to me at the time, I had broken my collarbone and second rib. Now, a year and a half later, climbing into the SUV, I slammed the door shut and thought, *This is the second time I'm leaving Gillette Stadium—broken.*

I sat for a minute, key in the ignition, eyes glued to the windshield. I wasn't looking at anything specific, just thinking. *Did that really just happen? God, I thought we were in this together! I thought we had a plan, a purpose! We were supposed to do some great things here!*

On and on these split-second thoughts blasted their way through my brain with fury. Finally, I unfroze.

I picked up my phone and called my brother Robby, or my friend Erik, maybe both. I can't remember. But they graciously arranged an immediate conference call with my circle of trust (#meettheparents). My family (Mom and Dad, sisters Christy and Katie, brothers Robby and Peter) and a few close friends rounded out this amazing bunch. While I needed to lean into their support, I also didn't want to have to share the same news twenty different times. I'm not a big fan of repeating myself, especially when it's bad news.

As I made the fifteen-minute drive through the back roads of Foxborough to the hotel, I told my loved ones the Patriots let me go. Heartfelt condolences, words of support, and what I needed most, prayer, poured out.

"I'm so sorry, Timmy."

"This is not over."

"God's got a plan."

And then together, we worked our way through what I would post on social media. How do you respond publicly to such a personal loss? What do you say? After much thought and reflection, I tweeted on August 31, 2013, 12:16 p.m.:

I would like to thank Mr. Kraft, Coach Belichick, Coach McDaniels and the entire Patriots organization for giving me the opportunity to be a part of such a classy organization. I pray for nothing but the best for you all. I will remain in relentless pursuit of continuing my lifelong dream of being an NFL quarterback. 2 Corinthians 12:9: "And He has said to me, 'My grace is sufficient for you, for power is perfected in weakness.' Most gladly, therefore, I will rather boast about my weaknesses, so that the power of Christ may dwell in me."

I was trying to mean every word. I really was. I knew in my heart it was true, but my emotions kept trying to override that.

That afternoon, not having the energy or the will to face a barrage of reporters or disappointed fans that were sure to flood the airport, a friend graciously offered to send a private plane that was already nearby and fly me to Jacksonville, where my parents lived. Since Mom and Dad weren't around, having previously committed to attend an event somewhere in Michigan, I planned to spend the rest of the day at Bryan's house with Robby. I had nowhere else to go. I'd been living in hotel rooms and rented apartments for the last few years. In fact, most of my stuff was in storage from the last cut.

When Bryan picked me up, I was pretty upset, quiet. Definitely no smile on my face. As I neared the car, I could hear loud bass thumping. Weird. Bryan's not really a bass-thumping kind of guy. When I opened the passenger door to hop in, the speakers blared at full volume Miley Cyrus's song "Party in the USA." Bryan smiled sheepishly as Miley belted out lyrics that mentioned feeling pressure and homesick and finally okay after hearing a Jay-Z song. I had to laugh. Out loud.

Once at Bryan's, I knew I wouldn't be able to leave for a while. I'd be blasted by media and others about being released. People were already giving their two cents about the decision, both spewing hate and offering encouragement on social media, blogs, and of course, every sports-media outlet. One source said I failed to take advantage of a great opportunity. Another said no one wanted me. And let's not forget the thousands upon thousands of critical comments and finger-pointing that followed each news blast.

As I walked through the front door of Bryan's beautiful home, my mind raced back to April 2010. The house had swarmed with family and close friends who munched on chicken fingers and mac and cheese while the seventy-fifth NFL draft blared on a large flat-screen TV. I can't tell you for how many years my brothers and I had watched the draft together at Bryan's house, but this was the first time we were waiting to hear my name.

Moments before the genesis of my professional football career was announced to the world, I took a call in Bryan's home office, shutting the door to drown out the excited background chatter. It was the Denver Broncos coach, Josh McDaniels. The team was about to choose me. I was officially a Bronco.

Now three and a half years later, I walked into that same house under much different circumstances. No party. No cheering. No high-fives. And definitely no chicken fingers or mac and cheese.

I gave Bryan's wife a hug. She looked at me with tears in her eyes and, not knowing what else to say, whispered in my ear, "We love you, Timmy." Bryan, Robby, and I crashed in Bryan's room. Remote control in hand, I flipped to the obvious choice—football. I have a joy in watching the game, especially college football, that just might be unrivaled by anyone. It's always been that way.

But that night, watching Clemson crush Georgia and highlights from other games, I realized my heart wasn't in it. One of the things in my life usually guaranteed to bring me joy was not, in that moment, cutting it at all. It was the first and only time I couldn't stomach watching football. I'm sure it didn't help that during every game and on every sports channel, the ticker kept running like a broken record: "Tebow gets released from the Patriots." We all saw it, but no one said a word. Why comment on the obvious? Wouldn't do me any favors.

"Hey, Bryan," I said. "Can you please find something else to watch?" I'm sure my tone betrayed annoyance.

"Sure, man," he nodded knowingly and started channel-surfing. Hundreds of shows and movies, and nothing to watch. First-world problems right there.

We finally settled on some movie. Though I fought so hard not to think, talk about it, or replay the conversation with my former coaches a thousand times in my head, it was hard not to. My mind and heart were elsewhere. While the film played, and with Bryan to the right and Robby to the left, piping up with funny or sarcastic commentary now and then, I fought an internal battle.

When your world is shaken, when the plans and dreams you've created, perhaps even banked on, get obliterated, when the path on which you walk is moving in an unknown and a particularly unwanted direction, what do you do? Better yet, what do you hold on to? I knew in that moment, I had to hold on to truth. It was the only solid ground I had. I had to remember what God said.

And I would have to do this over and over and over again.

I brought to mind Bible verses that I was taught growing up and that I've held on to over the years, like Jeremiah 29:11: "'For I know the plans that I have for you,' declares the LORD, 'plans for welfare and not for calamity to give you a future and a hope." And Psalm 56:3: "When I am afraid, I will put my trust in You."

I remembered the things my mom had always said to encourage me when I was down, like "God has big plans for you, Timmy; just wait on Him."

It was late when the flick ended. I'll never forget what happened when the ending credits rolled. Robby got up to return a phone call. Bryan got up to say good night to his wife. In other words, life was moving on for them. Their dailies were unchanged. Normal. Steady. Secure.

And for me, sitting on the edge of the bed, watching my friend's family cockapoo dart around my feet in wild figure eights yapping to no end, it felt like my world had exploded.

What am I going to do? What am I going to be? What am I going to strive for?

I don't put a lot of chips in different bags. I was devoted and committed to a career as a quarterback in the NFL. Period. End of story.

I prayed, my words weaving between questions and faith, doubt and surety. *God, I don't know what's happening, and I don't have a clue what You are doing, but I believe You have me here for a reason. I believe You've got a plan. I know this is not the end of my story. I may not be ecstatic about what You have in mind, but I'm in this with You. Whatever happens, I'm in.*

Though I carried the crushing weight of disappointment, I was working so hard to reenergize myself with confidence. Not in myself. Not in my abilities or my athleticism. I was drawing inner strength in whose I was. In the One who created me. In the One who loved me beyond all love.

Sometime that night I got on the phone with one of my agents. A few things happened when we talked. "Timmy, a bunch of teams are calling and hoping you'll play for them," he started, before rattling off the names of this one and that one. I was starting to get my hopes up, feeling a bit better.

My agent continued, trying to keep the momentum going. "So this one wants you to play tight end. That one wants you as an HB . . ." His voice trailed off. No mention of quarterback.

While every offer he told me about had really big selling points, I wasn't passionate about any of them. Know this: my attitude wasn't centered on arrogance. I wanted to continue to fight for what I *was* passionate about, for what I believed in. Since I was six years old, I didn't just want to play football; I wanted to be a quarterback. I didn't want to be in the NFL for the sake of being in it, or to make a lot of money, or to get famous. I wanted to pursue my passion of playing as a quarterback. To me, that was worth fighting for more than just making it in the NFL. I wanted to strive for my dream, not let others define me or my future.

So thanks, truly, truly, thank you, but no thanks.

My agent also gave me strict orders to stay under the radar. The biggest distraction to being on a team is attracting a media circus, something I've been told I have a tendency to do. This meant saying no to opportunities, appearances, and endorsements. And this meant basically doing nothing that could generate a paycheck. Well, I wasn't going to sit around all day and twiddle my thumbs.

I remembered Tom Brady once telling me about Tom House, whom I had met sometime previously in a roundabout way. House left quite an impression on me. He was crazy—in a good way. A fierce trainer who tutors athletes on mechanics and also pitched in the baseball major leagues for eight years, Tom was someone I knew I needed.

Sometime before the call with Tom House, and even while on it, pulling from the series of mental conversations I'd had since getting cut, I made a conscious choice not to quit. Not to gripe. Not to pout. Not to let others define me. And not to live in disappointment or regret. Believe me when I tell you, I wanted to be angry! And I was tempted to stay in that place. But I had to go back to the place of trusting God.

So I made the choice, on purpose, to put in the hard work of training while lying low. I was going to work with House, the best of the best. I knew my effort might not pay off in the way I wanted. I knew I might not make it in the NFL as a quarterback, but no one in the world was ever going to out-work me. I didn't know exactly what lay ahead, but I continually made the choice to trust God with the plan while doing my part and putting in the work. It wasn't easy and I didn't necessarily feel good about it, but I did it.

I can't tell you how many people around me recommended that I take a break. "Take some time off," they said in a hundred different ways. "You've worked so hard, at least rest for a week." But I couldn't. Taking a break wasn't in my vocabulary or my mind-set. Oh sure, in theory, taking a break sounded awesome. I would have loved to rest and just hang out with my family. But instead of what I wanted to do or even felt like doing, I chose to work. I chose to train. I chose to keep going and fight tooth and nail for my dream.

My agent made a phone call that night. And two days later I was in Los Angeles, where I'd stay for about eighteen months, training with Tom House at the University of Southern California. I'd live in someone's spare bedroom. I'd walk past students, professors, and members of the community, some of whom would come up to me, pity in their eyes, and say, "I'm sorry." Others would simply ask for a picture or an autograph. And then there were those who would offer unsolicited feedback and opinions of what I shouldn't have done or should have done and what they believed with pretty strong conviction I should do with my life.

But I'm getting ahead of things.

That night, after Robby walked out to make a phone call and Bryan went to see his wife, and as I was fighting for my future, I couldn't avoid the truth in the present. The ugly reality.

I had no job. No car. No home.

I'd let down the people who looked up to me.

No team wanted me to do what I'd dreamed of doing since I was little boy.

What exactly did the future hold?

I hadn't a clue.

2

WHO AM I?

**There is no greater discovery than seeing
God as the author of your destiny.**

—RAVI ZACHARIAS

Being cut hurt. No doubt, being told I couldn't do something that I loved doing and was so passionate about—playing quarterback—left me shaken.

So what do you do when life shakes you?

When your health fails . . .

When you lose your job . . .

When you get divorced . . .

When your dream flops . . .

When you make that one bad decision . . .

What do you do when something that has defined you your entire life is gone?

When your platform disappears . . .

When your perfect family is torn apart . . .

When you go bankrupt . . .

When your looks fade . . .

In tough moments like these, it's easy to question who we are. When my NFL career was crumbling, at times I'd wonder the same thing. *Am I the person who won the Heisman Trophy? Or am I the person who has been told over and over by so-called analysts that I can't throw?*

The dictionary defines *identity* as "who someone is, the name of a person, the qualities, beliefs, etc., that make a particular person or group different from others." I like to say that identity comes not necessarily from who we are, but from *whose* we are.

I am a child of God. My foundation for who I am is grounded in my faith. In a God who loves me. In a God who gives me purpose. In a God who sees the big picture. In a God who always has a greater plan.

Who am I? I am the object of His love.

That's a big deal. It's important to take God's love personally, though it may not be an easy thing to do. Sure, God loves the world, but He also loves each one of us individually. With billions of people on the planet, I know it can be hard to comprehend His love for us personally. God is infinite and lavishly shares His love with you and me. He can't spread Himself too thin. He cannot exhaust Himself. He cannot overextend Himself. And so every single person on the planet is the object of His love. Pretty incredible, right?

Love has been described as "the greatest and purest essence of who a person is and its proper expression brings fulfillment."[1] God doesn't choose to love. It's His nature, His essence, His being. "God is love."[2] It's what motivates His every move, inspires His action. It's a reflection of His heart, His character. God was love even before creation, because He has always been part of an eternal community of love: the Father, the Son, and the Holy Spirit.[3]

God's love is nothing like what we see depicted in the movies or even in our lives. Our fallen human nature typically evidences love as something we *do* in order to *get*—a "What's in it for me?" attitude. Or something we do in order to experience a particular feeling, a feeling that's fickle and fleeting. Or something that can be easily manipulated, dialed up or dialed down. God's love is nothing like this. His love is pure. It never fails. It is unconditional. It is eternal. It is not motivated by personal gain. He just loves because He is. It's worth noting that "unconditional love does not mean that God loves everything we do, but rather His love is so intense that He loves every sinner, no matter how vile and despicable he or she may be in the eyes of humanity."[4]

We can know we are special when we see the difference between God's love and human love. Coaches might love us because we score touchdowns. Your girlfriend might love you because you're the quarterback of the football team. Your friend might love you because you're funny and always there for him. But would they die for you? Would they give up their lives so that you could live? That's what Jesus did. He didn't just say He would die for us; He actually *did*.

Jesus died for *you*. Did you get that? If you were the only person on this planet, He still would have died for you. That's some powerful stuff!

Knowing I am the object of His love lays the groundwork for who I am. I am wanted. I am adopted into His family. I belong. A sense of belonging is a basic human need, just like food and water. We all want to feel loved and accepted. This is why middle and high schools are full of different cliques and groups. And this is why many attach themselves to the jocks, the musicians, the overachievers, the theater crew, the rebels, or the popular crowd.

But who I am is not based on others, on fitting in, on belonging to a certain crowd, or on living a certain lifestyle. My identity is based on belonging to God. No one can take this foundation away from me. I know this to be true, and while I often need to be reminded, I aim to live by these truths every day.

There have been times when I was playing football that my identity was muddled. But there have also been times when I felt so grounded in whose I was that nothing else mattered. I can say that when I'm living in the right perspective, when I am clearheaded in my identity and not clouded by the judgment of others or by my perceived abilities, I live at my best.

If people like me, I will strive to know whose I am. If people don't like me, I will still strive to know whose I am. If I play football, I will strive to know whose I am. If I never play again, I'll still strive to know whose I am. Whether I'm praised or criticized, popular or outcast, rich or poor, I will always strive to remember that I belong. That I am loved. That I am a child of God.

Trust me, when you know whose you are, it changes everything. Henri Nouwen put it this way:

> Your true identity is as a child of God. This is the identity you have to accept. Once you have claimed it and settled in it, you can live in a world that gives you much joy as well as pain. You can receive the praise as well as the blame that comes to you as an opportunity for strengthening your basic identity, because the identity that makes you free is anchored beyond all human praise and blame. You belong to God, and it is as a child of God that you are sent into the world.[5]

Stop and think for a moment. What defines you? What are you known for? What do you do or what have you done that might make up your identity?

Is it money? Friendships? Status? Power? Social-media followers?

I can tell you that money comes and goes. I've had a lot in my bank account and next to nothing. And friendships? It's amazing to look back and see how many people reached out to me when my NFL career was at an all-time high versus the times I got cut. Popularity, much like money and anything else, ebbs and flows. Status? That changes too.

I know failure is something that defines a lot of people. I could have easily allowed the lows in my life to influence my identity. I've failed a lot of people. I've made a lot of mistakes. I've thought the wrong things. I've wondered how God could even use me. But just as I try not to let the trophies, the wins, the awards, the magazine covers, or the accolades I've earned and experienced define me, I also try not to let the bottom points in my life tell me who I am. I just know that God is on my side. And with Him, all things are possible.

Because my identity is secure, I don't have to ride the roller coaster of life. I don't have to live up in the highs or down in the lows. No matter what happens I can live with confidence knowing I'm on a solid foundation.

I've won two national championships and a Heisman Trophy, and I've been released from, oh, just a few NFL teams.

I've been praised by presidents and had congressional bills passed in my honor, and I've also been shredded mercilessly in the media.

I've been celebrated in rap songs and the butt of jokes on TV shows.

I've been wooed by celebrities, and I may or may not have had a, well, not very uplifting song written about me by a famous musician.

And while I may get hurt, disappointed, or frustrated by the negative side of these equations, my foundation doesn't have to change. Even if I wrestle with internal feelings, I can hold on to God's truth. I can flow north again. I know He's got a plan for me, even when I don't know what it is or when it seems to look totally different than what I imagined.

This is what identity is about.

ROCK STAR

Mark Stuart, former lead singer for Audio Adrenaline, knows what it feels like to have your identity shaken by the unexpected.

Eight studio albums selling over three million copies.

Seventeen number-one radio hits.

Two Grammys.

Multiple Dove awards.

At their peak, Audio Adrenaline enjoyed the kind of success that struggling musicians only dream about. The kind of momentum that pushes you to ride the wave. To create more music. To produce more hits.

Artists don't usually end their careers at the height of success. That doesn't seem like the smartest thing to do. But for lead front-man Mark Stuart, he didn't have much of a choice. In 2004, while singing to a crowd of young, devoted fans who had followed the band for years, Mark noticed something different with his voice. It didn't sound like it always had. Something was wrong.

At first, he didn't do anything about it. Mark tried hiding it, intentionally writing songs so the band's guitarist could sing lead vocals. He also made self-deprecating jokes about sounding cooler, more like Bryan Adams or Rod Stewart. But with each passing concert and time spent in the studio, Mark knew he had a serious problem.

Regular visits with the top doctors in the country proved pointless. Nobody could tell Mark what was wrong. Specialists scoped the singer's vocal cords and couldn't come up with a diagnosis. For three years, Mark was in and out of doctors' offices to find out why he was losing his voice. He relied heavily on steroid shots just to get through his heavy touring schedule. Eventually the shots became ineffective, and Mark lost hope of ever getting his voice back. He admits that during this time, the joy of being on stage was fading. And then, people began to notice. He couldn't hide any longer.

Ultimately diagnosed with spasmodic dysphonia, an incurable disorder where the muscles in the voice box spasm, Mark officially stepped down as the lead singer of Audio Adrenaline in 2006. No more singing. No more concerts. No more touring.

Despite having an amazing seventeen-year run with the band, the former rock star struggled at first to accept that he couldn't do any longer what he was so passionate about, what he thought he was born to do.

Mark admits to feeling numb during this time, feeding his tendency to isolate himself from others and draw inward. He admits to living in moments where he wondered, *What am I going to do?* He admits to feeling torn, sometimes accepting that God was in control, orchestrating the unknown in a better and bigger plan, and sometimes wondering what he could do himself to change his circumstances.

When I recently talked to Mark as I was working on this book, I was amazed to learn how grounded he has been for most of his life. He was the same person at the height of his music career, when his fan base grew and album sales soared, as when he was a struggling musician, not knowing how or even if his career would take off.

Mark's identity was still secure, seventeen years later, when he had to literally sign off on leaving the band, saying good-bye to something he had worked so hard to create, to build, to sustain.

"God was authoring a bigger picture," Mark told me. "He always gets you to where He wants you to be in spite of yourself."

I told Mark how much I loved their early hit "Big House," a song in which they described what heaven would be like. In fact, I got excited about heaven because of it. Even when I was a little boy, that song fueled in me a passion to do things for eternity, to do stuff that mattered in the big picture.

And yeah, maybe a part of the reason I loved the song so much was because of the chorus, the part where Mark sang something about playing football up there. This catchy tune put Audio Adrenaline on the map and later was even named song of the decade in the nineties.[6] What a lot of people don't know is that the song was inspired by a Haitian children's song Mark heard while on a mission trip in that part of the world.

Mark fell in love with Haiti as a teenager while his parents were serving as missionaries in the north-coast town of Saint-Louis du Nord. Throughout college and the early years of Audio Adrenaline, Mark regularly visited this country to serve with his family. But after the release of their hit song "Hands and Feet," Mark and the band felt called to do more than just sing about serving; they wanted to get their hands dirty. Moved to act in light of the growing number of orphans saturating the Haitian population, the band created the Hands and Feet Project, an organization that still helps fight to keep families together and to meet the needs of Haiti's orphan and abandoned children.

When Mark left the band, he devoted his life, still using the band's platform, to care for those who were helpless.

I admire Mark so much. A forward thinker, he is actually working with the Haitian government to rewrite that country's cultural narrative. He is helping to create jobs and in turn give back to the economy. He is doing this not to make money, build fame, or reinvent a new name for himself, but so others can have hope.

When I first met Mark a few years back, I was drawn to his vision for children with special needs. He told me there are only a few orphanages in Haiti that take in kids with disabilities. Most of them don't even make it to one of those orphanages. It is a common belief in Haitian society that babies who are born with special needs are cursed. Many of these children are discarded, abandoned at hospitals, and in some cases literally thrown away in the trash. My foundation has since partnered with Hands and Feet. We're combining our visions to help build a medical clinic as well as a children's home that helps kids with special needs get adopted.

While he is no longer on a stage, accompanied by a microphone and surrounded by talented musicians, Mark is still making a difference. He is not bitter. He does not mourn the loss of his voice. He does not miss the limelight. Mark is doing things beyond himself.

He told me, "God fills up so much of my life with good things that I don't miss what I don't have anymore."

Mark is often approached by people asking if they can pray for him. They also ask questions like "Do you want to be healed?" "Do you want your voice back?" and "Don't you want to sing again?"

The answer is always the same. "God has already healed me. I lost my voice as a singer so I can be a voice for these kids." Mark has not allowed a significant loss to define who he is. He is more than a rock star. More than a performer. More than a singer. He is fulfilling a greater purpose. He is part of a greater plan.

Who's on Your Team?

On March 28, 1990, the Chicago Bulls traveled to Richfield Coliseum to play the Cleveland Cavaliers. Michael Jordan dominated. In overtime, he led his team to a hard-fought victory, 117–113. Scoring a career high of sixty-nine points in that game, Jordan was unstoppable, bloodthirsty, a reckoning force. This was probably one of his most legendary performances.

That night there was another, lesser-known player for the Bulls, rookie Stacey King. King took four shots and missed each one. But on the fourth, he got fouled. Picture with me the scene. Imagine the stress King feels walking to the free-throw line. The crowd is going wild. All eyes are on him.

Pressure's on. Beads of sweat drip down his cheek as he focuses, dribbling, getting ready to shoot. *I've got to do my part,* he thinks. *I've got to help my guys win this.*

He looks over and sees his teammate Michael Jordan, the best player in the NBA. Think King feels somewhat insecure? He releases the ball; it flies toward the hoop, then clangs off the rim. Miss. He prepares for his second shot. Cavs fans are on their feet, arms waving in the air. More pressure. But this time, the *swish* of the ball through the net echoes throughout the stadium. *Good!* Game over! The crowd wilts and walks—grumbling—to the exits.

After the game, the press bombard Michael Jordan in the locker room. As reporters cram around the guy trying to get a quote, someone, who probably couldn't get close enough to Jordan, started talking to Stacey King and asking him questions. At one point in the postgame commentary, King quipped, "I'll always remember this as the night that Michael Jordan and I combined to score 70 points."[7]

That's pretty funny, considering King only scored one point. But in the big picture, who cares? The win was a combined effort. Michael Jordan was an extraordinary teammate to have. What would it be like to have him on your basketball team? Pretty awesome, right? It's practically impossible to lose!

Now imagine God being on your team. Imagine what's possible. Imagine what that could look like.

When who you are is grounded in whose you are, you realize it doesn't matter what life throws your way. When your world starts to shake or fall apart, you can lean into Him for security, for safety. You can get through even the toughest of circumstances because God is on your side. He loves you more than you know. And He's got everything under control more than you know. He's got plans for you. Awesome plans! You and God are unstoppable!

PURPOSE

God created you for a reason. He created you to be special. He created you for a purpose. Imagine there is no God. Then you were not created for a reason. You aren't special. You are the accidental, unintentional result of motion, matter, time, and chance. Tim Keller said, "If your origin is insignificant and your destiny is insignificant, which means someday nobody will even remember anything you ever did, have the guts to admit your life is insignificant."[8]

Purpose is one of those words that people have tossed around so much, especially in Christian circles, that it's hard to know exactly what it means. Is it this one grand event that unfolds when you're at the right place at the right time? Is it something that you are passionate about or what you are naturally skilled at doing? Is it doing something that makes you happy? Does it have anything to do with helping others? While I'm not a theologian or a Bible expert and can't offer you a five-step plan to finding your purpose, I believe that it's intertwined with your identity.

A man named Paul, one of the earliest church missionaries, wrote, "For we are His workmanship, created in Christ Jesus for good works, which God prepared beforehand so that we would walk in them" (Ephesians 2:10).

The Greek word for "workmanship" is *poiema,* or "poem." Think about this. Before you were even born, God wrote a beautiful poem about your life. This masterpiece is about you doing not just meaningless or average things, but good works, wonderful things that make a difference. This means that you are important, significant. You matter!

When life gets tough, when your relationship starts to fall apart, when the cancer comes back, when you can't beat the addiction, when your kids are running wild, when your parents are driving you crazy, when you feel stuck in monotony or routine, it's important to circle back to God's love and the fact that He has an amazing purpose for your life. This is something I've needed to do consistently in order to encourage myself. Remember the last chapter? When no team wanted me as their quarterback, I had to keep reminding myself over and over that God has a purpose. That He has a plan. Some days it was easy to believe; other days it was a struggle.

I don't know what your purpose is. Maybe it's to become a doctor and help cure cancer. Maybe it's to be a parent and shepherd your family. Maybe it's to become an entrepreneur and partner with a nonprofit organization. It might be to help children all over the world or just your own, one million people or just one.

I remember reading a great story of how an American missionary named Sam Wolgemuth spoke to hundreds of young people at a rally in New Delhi, India. After preaching his heart out, pouring his soul into these lives through his message, he invited those who wanted to trust in Jesus to come forward to the front of the platform.

Only one person did. I imagine Sam was disappointed by the lack of response. I imagine he hoped to see more lives changed, impacted by the message of the Good News. But this man, the only one who responded in commitment to Jesus, became one of the most well-known and respected Christian apologists of all time, Dr. Ravi Zacharias.[9]

Regardless of how your life will impact others and what that will look like, I just know that when your identity is grounded in God, when you trust in Him, you become part of a bigger picture. And you begin to live out this wonderful poem He has written for your life. This is the truth when life is smooth sailing, and this is the truth when storms come.

And trust me, they will.

BUT . . .

You are unique. You are valuable. And you matter.

Do you find this hard to believe? I hope not. But if you do, I'd like to encourage you.

I can't tell you how many people I've met who struggle with doubt. I'm going to get into this in more detail in chapter 5, but it's worth mentioning here. Some have admitted to me that they feel they have nothing to offer because of mistakes they've made. Some feel they have nothing to contribute skill-wise, money-wise, or talent-wise. Some feel like they're too old, others too young.

Whatever you may struggle with—and all of us struggle with something—in not having enough or anything good enough, know this: With Jesus, you have everything. With Him, you have what it takes to fulfill a purpose. You may not have graced the covers of fashion magazines, you may not have a million dollars in the bank, you may not be Tom Brady or Michael Jordan or Taylor Swift or Chris Tomlin or Mother Teresa, but you have something. And with God, that's more than enough.

Whether you're a stay-at-home mom struggling to stay afloat in the midst of diapers and feedings, whether you're a third-year college student and still have no idea what you want to do with your life, whether you're stuck in a dead-end job eight hours a day, know that God is a big God. And He can do for you what He did for a little boy thousands of years ago.

You may have heard this story a hundred times if you grew up in Sunday school, or this might be your first time reading about it. After a long day of teaching and ministering to others, sharing with many lives the message of the Good News, Jesus and His disciples are ready for a break. They need a breather. So He takes them on a boat ride to the opposite side of the lake where together they climb up a hill. I imagine they're all exhausted. Probably a little emotionally spent too, and looking forward to some downtime. But it quickly turns out that this is not going to be a time to recharge. The crowds come. And fast. They want to see Jesus. While some had heard about Him through the grapevine, some had actually seen Him do extraordinary things. Like make the blind see. Make the lame walk. Make the deaf hear. I'm sure there were those who sought Jesus out of curiosity and others out of need.

The crowd grows in number. This was more than just a handful of people. The hillside swarms with men, women, and children—they just keep coming. The Bible tells us the disciples counted five thousand men that day. Now, that's not considering the number of women and children present, which some scholars suggest would likely have increased that number to at least double.

It's getting late. Close to dinnertime. Seeing the crowd, Jesus asks, "Where can we buy food to feed everyone?"[10] It's an interesting question, especially because there wasn't a Sam's Club or Costco or any other retail warehouse giant down the other side of the hill. Not to mention, Jesus and His crew weren't rich and couldn't afford to foot the bill for ten-thousand-plus meals.

And here is where it starts to get good.

We don't know his name. We don't know how he managed to get the attention of one of Jesus's disciples. We don't know his story, his background, his education, his family life, or his worldview. All we know is that a little boy in the crowd noticed a problem and gave what he had, his own meal, five loaves of bread and two fish, to help fix it.

I wonder if the kid wrestled with his decision to give what he had. Maybe he was embarrassed that what he had to offer was not a lot. Maybe he was even afraid Jesus would poke fun at him. I mean, really, what on earth can you do with five loaves of bread and two fish? I may not be a mathematician, but I know how to divide. And five loaves and two fish is not enough food to feed ten thousand people. It could be that he was shy, nervous, and that as he looked over at the guy next to him, the one holding a bigger dinner, was tempted to hoard his own, assuming the other guy would share. Or maybe, just maybe, the boy instantly felt moved in his heart to give. Maybe he intuitively knew that if anyone could do something with what little he had, Jesus was the guy.

And I wonder what Jesus's disciple thought as he held this boy's meal in his hands. Did he shake his head in disbelief? Laugh? Tell the kid "thank you" out loud but in his mind ridicule him for his pitiable contribution? We know at least one of the disciples doesn't seem entirely grateful for it. Andrew tells Jesus, "There's a young boy here with five barley loaves and two fish. But what good is that with this huge crowd?"[11] Andrew may not have necessarily appreciated the meal, but let's be real, would you have? Would I?

Jesus did.

"Tell everyone to sit down,"[12] He says. Then after waiting for the crowd to get situated, He prays for what they are about to eat. I imagine it doesn't take long before five loaves of bread and two fish run out, but they never do. Not only does every single person on the hillside that day eat dinner; there are twelve baskets full of leftovers.

Not just enough. More than enough.

You can take away so many lessons from this story, but the one thing that strikes me is how God can do a lot with what we think is a little. How He can take something that can be described as "insignificant" or "not enough" or "small" or "meaningless" and use it to perform a miracle. He can do the same with you. It didn't matter if the boy had five loaves or five thousand loaves, the amount is not the point. God doesn't want your stuff. He wants your heart. It doesn't matter if you don't think it's good enough.

No matter how many stupid things we've done, He doesn't look at us as stupid. No matter how many times we've failed, He doesn't look at us as failures. No matter how many foolish things we've done, He doesn't look at us as fools. When we are willing to let God shape our identity, He will take whatever we have to offer and multiply it in ways and for a purpose that we cannot even begin to imagine.

Sometimes we get stuck in this purpose thing because of our baggage. Many of us carry our guilt, our pain, and our mistakes around for years. Because we can't even begin to think of ourselves in a good way, we don't believe that God can. We think if we can't forgive ourselves that God never will. We think if we can't see a different, better future for ourselves than what's staring us in the face, God never will. What we have to realize is that God's ability to love and forgive and restore is not the same as ours. Why?

> "For My thoughts are not your thoughts,
> Nor are your ways My ways," declares the LORD.
> "For as the heavens are higher than the earth,
> So are My ways higher than your ways
> And My thoughts than your thoughts." (Isaiah 55:8–9)

Think about this. If we can understand everything about the God we serve, what kind of god would that be? If we could figure Him out, grasp His every move, and package Him neatly with the right labels, He wouldn't be that great. Or powerful. Or abounding in knowledge and wisdom.

But God is so much more than we could ever imagine. He has no limits. He offers us more love, more kindness, more grace, and more forgiveness than we could conceive of on our own.

I get so excited just thinking about that. Probably because I need it!

It's Not Over

"Why No One in the NFL Wants Tim Tebow."

"Chip Kelly: Tim Tebow Not 'Good Enough' to Be Our Third-Stringer."

"Is It Finally Over for Tim Tebow?"

Ouch. It can be pretty easy to read headlines like these—and there are a whole lot more—and start to believe the lie that the best is over. There were definitely times in the past few years when I thought I'd never play ball again. But you know what I've learned? My best days are not behind me. They are in front of me. This reminds me of Stephen Covey's personal motto: "Live life in crescendo! Your most important work is always ahead of you."[13]

What about you? What are you going through right now that is so crushing you think you'll never get past it? What are you dealing with that makes you think your best is gone? Are you wondering how you are going to get over that failure? That heartbreak? That illness? That class you failed? That addiction? Hear my heart. My intention is not to minimize your pain or struggle. The tough times and trials we go through are real and painful. I get that. My hope is to encourage you in the midst of them.

It's not over for you. Wherever you are in life, this can be a beginning.

When Mark Stuart left Audio Adrenaline, many worried the move was going to ruin his legacy. But he wasn't concerned. "The legacy for me is leaving something behind that is bigger than the band, like the Hands and Feet ministry."

Sometimes I wonder if Mark and I would have ever connected if he hadn't lost his voice and my NFL career had gone in a different direction. Who knows? But then I think about the result that came about because of what happened. Instead of singing on stage and instead of scoring touchdowns right now, Mark and I are fighting for those who can't fight for themselves. It may not be what I originally had in mind, but God's infinite love and knowledge are better than my wants or my plans.

Don't worry about your skills or what you lack. Don't worry about your past junk. Don't worry about what you lost. Don't worry about what lies ahead. Don't worry about what didn't happen or what did. Be rooted in God. And watch as He unfolds a plan that has more love, more meaning, and more purpose than you could ever possibly imagine.

3

FACING THE GIANTS

Fear is a self-imposed prison that will keep you from becoming what God intends for you to be. You *must* move against it with the weapons of faith and love.

—Rick Warren

A fourth-quarter-comeback team. This was the reputation the Denver Broncos were beginning to earn in 2011. I can tell you about game after game after game where the odds were stacked against us and winning looked improbable. But we never stopped believing we could win. And at the eleventh hour, we pulled through.

Like when we faced the Miami Dolphins on October 23, 2011. In my first game as a starter, although I was giving my all, it wasn't necessarily my best. On my first eleven drives, I was 4 for 14 for 40 yards and zero touchdowns, and I was sacked seven times. With 5:23 on the clock, the Dolphins (did I mention they were 0–5?) had a 15-point lead. We had 0 points. Pretty embarrassing.

But then, we got the ball back.

Together we were able to move the ball down the field with a touchdown pass to Demaryius Thomas. Then, another touchdown pass to Daniel Fells.

In a play that tied the game and put us in overtime, I ran in a 2-point conversion on a quarterback draw. We shut down the Dolphins with a field goal, 18–15. It was the largest deficit overcome in a victory with less than three minutes since the 1970 NFL merger.[1]

And then there was the game against the Chicago Bears on December 11 that same year. For just under one hour, the Bears had us in their pocket. I finished the first quarter 3 of 7 passing for 45 yards and one interception to Chicago's Charles Tillman. In the second quarter, I was 0 for 6. The third quarter was just as bad, 0 for 3. Not a very good start, and it wasn't looking like a good end to the game. By the time the fourth quarter rolled around, the Bears led 10–0.

With five minutes and fourteen seconds on the clock, it was turnaround time. Completing 9 of 14 passes for 85 yards, I led my team on a 7-play, 63-yard drive that Demaryius Thomas took home for a touchdown.

When the two-minute warning came, we were down a field goal. With Chicago running out of bounds, and without any time-outs on our side, eventually I helped move the ball to a game-tying field goal with three seconds left. In overtime, Matt Prater took it home on a 51-yard kick to lead our team to a 13–10 win over the stunned Bears.

Under Pressure

Some people get better in the fourth quarter, and some don't. Pressure can paralyze, especially toward the end of a game when you're faced with the sheer fact that winning, statistically speaking, does not look likely. But those kinds of odds fire me up. I've always liked winning this way.

As a little boy, I never dreamed about winning football games 45–0. I dreamed about being down six points, crushing it in the last few minutes of the game, and then having a crazy celebration with my teammates about the unimaginable win. Because that's what you remember in life, the special, unlikely moments, the comebacks, being dominated by pressure and overcoming.

Joe Montana isn't remembered for all the blowouts he had. He's remembered for his clutch moments. As a kid I watched many times the video of the play known as The Catch, when the 49ers played the Cowboys in 1982 and won the NFC Championship, 28–27, on a 6-yard pass from Montana to Dwight Clark with only 51 seconds left.

What's pressure? Another word for fear. It's fear that tells us, *You're not good enough.* Pressure can overcome many athletes in big moments. It can be easy to succumb to the fear and think, *I can't live up to the hype . . . I can't make this play in the crunch time . . . I can't perform under the bright lights when everyone is watching . . .*

Fear is a powerful emotion. It's something that controls a lot of people, not just athletes.

While playing with the Broncos, though I may have feared that I might not get the shot or that if we lost, my position would be taken away, I was always driven further by love. By the love I have for the game and for my teammates, for what we can make possible when we rally together.

Fear can push or motivate you to do things, sometimes even good things, but it will never take you as far as love can take you.

I think about my dad, a missionary, a man who has the most courage of anyone I've ever met. In 1985, he and my mom moved the family (nine-year-old Christy, seven-year-old Katie, four-year-old Robby, and one-year-old Peter) to the Philippines. He felt moved in his heart to serve the people of this country, which is made up of seven-thousand-plus islands. This was a time of political unrest when Communist insurgents known as the New People's Army were often at odds with and in violent conflicts against the Philippine government.

My family lived on the remote southern island of Mindanao. Two years later they moved to Manila, where I was born. When I was only a week old, Dad watched, shocked, as armed rebel forces rolled into a village in military tanks, the noise deafening, hoping to take over a local broadcast facility. Gunfire sounded in the streets as the government forces defended themselves against the insurgents. Needless to say, Dad came back quickly to our house. We gathered some personal belongings and evacuated immediately, taking refuge in a hotel.

That's pretty scary stuff. My dad has countless stories of how fear could have easily overtaken him. But it didn't. Why? Because his love for the people of the Philippines and, more importantly, his love for God were stronger than what he could have feared was possible. In fact, my mom recently told me that one time while Dad was preaching, someone holding a knife ran right behind where he was standing, holding his arm high in the air as if to attack Dad with the weapon. My father didn't even notice the guy. It took all of a few seconds before someone tackled the knife-wielding man. Dad, so engrossed in preaching and loving on the Filipinos, wasn't moved at all by the commotion.

I learned a lot about fear and love from my dad. While I was in the process of this unconventional upbringing, he taught us a lot of Scripture about fear—many verses that my mom put to song so that we would always remember that God is greater than anything we could possibly be afraid of.

Dad sacrificed so much to leave the States, move an entire family to a foreign country, and share the love of Jesus with people who couldn't do anything for him in return. There is something extremely powerful about that. This is love in action.

What fears overwhelm you? Are you afraid that others won't like you? Are you afraid that you'll miss the deadline? Are you afraid that you'll never get married? Are you afraid that you'll never find your purpose? And what are you feeding more? Your fears, or your love for a God who has promised to be faithful?

LOVE MATTERS

Love is not a feeling; it's a choice. It doesn't say, "I love you because you will do x, y, or z for me." The ultimate form of love is choosing the best interests of another regardless of how it affects us.

In the New Testament, there are at least three different Greek words used for love: *storge,* which signifies a natural affection we feel toward our family (parents, siblings, children); *phileo,* "to show *warm affection* in intimate *friendship,* characterized by tender, heartfelt consideration and kinship"[2]; and *agape,* my favorite definition of which is "unconditional love that is always giving and impossible to take or be a taker. It devotes total commitment to seek your highest best no matter how anyone may respond. This form of love is totally selfless and does not change whether the love given is returned or not."[3] This is love that acts in the best interests of others, not your own.

When Jesus died for us, He evidenced agape love. Giving His life in return for our freedom from sin was a daunting task. In fact, on the night before He was to be crucified, He wrestled with God, His Father, while praying in the Garden of Gethsemane: "Father, if You are willing, remove this cup from Me."[4] It's evident His heart was torn between doing what He knew was necessary and being shadowed by the fear of what it required. In fact, the Bible says that Jesus "being in agony . . . was praying very fervently; and His sweat became like drops of blood, falling down upon the ground."[5]

Jesus wasn't in agony over a little something; He was sweating drops of blood. That is a big deal! While I'm sure He was partly afraid of the physical torture that was coming, there was a greater fear. His crucifixion also meant separation from God. He would bear the entire weight of the world, of my sin and yours, on the cross. And that meant that until His resurrection, His heavenly Father would turn His back on His Son. That perfect relationship would be severed. Physical torture is one thing, but abandonment can hurt even more.

So Jesus asked His Father if maybe, just maybe, there was another way. Yet He didn't park on that thought for a long time. Jesus's prayer quickly continued, and He ended His tear-filled plea with the following: "Yet not My will, but Yours be done."[6] *This is what needs to be done, so I'll do it.*

Fear doesn't make you give your life for someone else. Fear doesn't make you run into a burning building to save your child. Oh sure, you may high-tail it into that building afraid that something bad is going to happen to your kid, but your love for that child will overwhelm that fear. Fear doesn't make you take a bullet for someone. But love does. Let love dominate, the kind of love that we choose over our feelings, over peer pressure, over our selfish desires, over our fears, and over our disappointments.

When you want to be the most powerful or the strongest, always choose love over fear. "There is no fear in love; but perfect love casts out fear" (1 John 4:18).

THE FIGHTER

Prom. Graduation. College applications. Dates. Cars. Clothes. Just some of the things a typical high-school senior would be thinking about.

Except for Chelsie Watts.

In August 2011, after she had her appendix removed in an emergency surgery, she was diagnosed with appendiceal adenocarcinoma, a rare cancer diagnosis for someone her age. Instead of going to parties, hanging out with her friends at football games, and spending weekends at the mall or the movies, this girl went through chemotherapy and multiple surgeries. On July 5, 2012, Chelsie celebrated what she thought would be her last chemo infusion.

A year later, after she completed her freshman year at Stephen F. Austin State University in Texas, the cancer came back. This time, stronger than ever. With a quiet confidence and sweet spirit, Chelsie fought back. Though her body was weak and failing her, her faith was strong. And through more chemo and more surgeries, she held tight to her favorite verse, Psalm 27:1: "The Lord is my light and my salvation—whom shall I fear? The Lord is the stronghold of my life—of whom shall I be afraid?" (NIV).

By the time I met her in November 2014, she'd already had her appendix, uterus, ovaries, spleen, colon, gallbladder, and most of her small intestine removed. I was so taken by her strength. Despite being frail, she didn't come across as a victim of the cancer. Always having a genuine smile, she came across as a fighter.

Chelsie and I shared an amazing time together. I was honored to have her pampered at a spa for a day and show her behind-the-scenes action at *SEC Nation*. I'll never forget how her face beamed while the crowds chanted her name after I introduced her to the fans at Texas A&M University. Not a dry eye that day.

Chelsie radiated love, an unbending devotion to God, even while knowing her prognosis wasn't looking good. She told a reporter, "I know where I'm going to go. . . . I'm going to spend eternity in heaven without pain, without disease. And so I'm not scared."[7]

We kept in touch after that weekend. During our talks, it quickly became apparent that I wasn't the one encouraging Chelsie; she was always the one encouraging me. Chelsie was the one giving me the right perspective on life. She would always say, "God's got this," no matter what the medical reports said, no matter how many more surgeries or chemo sessions she had to go through, no matter what the doctors told her. She even wrote a song during this time. I love the chorus:

As the journey ended
I danced I learned I was healed
And if this should ever happen again I'll always know
When the road gets rough and it's gonna be hard
Don't give up cuz God's Got This

That's Chelsie for you. Confident and unwavering.

I'll never forget the end of January 2015, right before Super Bowl weekend. I was in Arizona, training, and felt all out of sorts. It was a crazy emotional or mental (or both) funk that I just couldn't shake. I didn't know where it was coming from. It was so bad I couldn't sleep for a few nights. Literally. The first night, no sleep. Second night, no sleep. By the third night, tossing and turning, feeling restless, still no sleep. This had never happened in my life! What was going on?

Finally, desperate for help after trying unsuccessfully to function on zero sleep, I went to visit my trainer. He whipped up a (legal) concoction of a bunch of different stuff. Let's just say it was so strong, it should have knocked me out for a day. My sister drove me home as I started getting sleepy. In that moment, I can't tell you how grateful I was to my trainer, knowing in a short time I'd finally be able to catch some z's. But once home, lying in bed, that same feeling of unease took over. So I prayed. Unfortunately, I can't say I took the focus off of myself and prayed for someone else who needed it. My prayers were all about Timmy-Timmy-Timmy, multiple variations of "Please, Jesus, let me sleep."

And then, my phone rang.

It was Brandi, a woman who works at our foundation and has one of the most beautiful and sweetest hearts of anyone I know. "Chelsie's taken a turn for the worst," she said softly. I immediately shot out of bed. After getting more specifics from Brandi, I found out Chelsie had started to deteriorate at the same time I had started having trouble sleeping. After hanging up with Brandi, I dialed Chelsie's number. Her mother answered, telling me in hushed tones that her daughter was too weak to talk but she would put the phone up to her ear so I could share a few things with her.

I could barely hear Chelsie's labored breathing as I prayed for and shared Scripture with her. "I'm proud of you, Chels. You've had such an impact on this world, and I know that God is proud of you too. You've been an amazing role model for me, for your family, for so many people. If you want to continue to fight, I'll be with you. I'll hop on a plane and see you in a few hours."

And, never before having said anything quite like this to anyone who had a life-threatening illness, I felt in my heart to say something else. "Chels, if you want to stop fighting, stop fighting and go home. Remember, you are leaving a legacy. You are amazing! And I love you."

It wasn't but an hour or two after that when I got another call from Brandi. Chelsie had passed away. My friend had fought the good fight. She had finished the race. She had kept the faith.[8]

Chelsie's mom says that her daughter's "courageous and grace-filled battle against cancer has had a profound effect on many lives. Within her demure demeanor was a mighty oak tree rooted in her faith, unwavering. Cancer never wins. God is bigger than this disease. No matter the outcome, healed by Him or taken home to live in eternity, we win." She calls her daughter a picture of hope. A fighter. A mighty warrior. And she's right. Chelsie was a warrior.

How do you live in such a place of hope, love, trust? How do you keep from feeling so overwhelmed by fear that you shut down? How do you keep from letting the giants in life pummel you to the ground? How do you, in the face of mountains and adversaries, stay grounded?

Faith.

WORK IT

"Faith is the assurance of things hoped for, the conviction of things not seen."[9] I like what Martin Luther King Jr. said: "Faith is taking the first step even when you don't see the whole staircase."[10] This doesn't mean never worrying, never being sad or disappointed. We're not robots. We're human beings with flesh and blood, minds, hearts, souls, and spirits. We feel things.

Faith is not being consumed with the emotions that come with the highs and lows while being able to grow in the process. Though you might feel afraid, sad, or disappointed, faith is not being shaken at your core but moving through your struggle one step at a time.

During one of my lows, a pastor who counsels me reminded me that God is always in the process of molding us. He encouraged me by saying that I was like a clay pot on the potter's wheel, my faith being crafted and shaped by God. This process is not easy. We are kneaded, shaped, molded, and flexed. And sometimes the end result isn't so great, so we need more kneading, shaping, molding, and flexing. And still, we may bear cracks and flaws, bumps and bruises. We're human, after all. We'll never reach perfection in this life. The point is to have our faith stretched and challenged and growing so we can show the world that no matter how many times we get knocked down or fall short, we can still hold on to God's promises. We can still believe that He has a better plan. We can still hold on to His truth. We can still hold on to His unfailing love.

Some might say that walking by faith is easy—or that it should be. It's not. Most things that are worth it aren't easy. Oh sure, think how easy it was for me to get super-pumped and put Bible verses on my eye black when I was winning championships and trophies and scoring touchdowns. It's easy to praise God when you're dominating the game. It's easy to praise God when you don't have any problems, when everyone likes you, when you're in perfect health, when the money is in the bank, when obstacles are nowhere to be seen. But when a giant stands in front of you—whether in the form of cancer or a career that's flopping—what does your faith look like then?

When I was cut from the Patriots, I was in the middle of a pretty intense devotional study with my friend Erik. Part of what we were doing each day was reading a portion of the Bible chronologically. I'll admit that after I was cut, I wasn't necessarily inspired to pick the Bible back up and keep reading. In fact, at times I just didn't want to do it. I said to myself, *I know this. I've already read this years ago. Why do I have to do it again?*

I wonder if I had still been on the team or starting, would I have had a better attitude? But just because subconsciously I may have been acting like a spoiled brat, that didn't mean I had to bench my faith. It meant I had to work it out, just like a muscle. While holding the Bible in my hand, feeling discouraged, at odds with myself, I remember thinking that I have to choose to believe that God still has a plan. As much as it hurt and as hard as it was, I had to keep choosing to believe that His plan is better than my plan. That God is still God. That He, somehow and in some way, is coming through. And I had to stop being a baby and to continue studying.

A lot of what it means to work out your faith muscle is to choose to live above your feelings, to remember that He is God and that you are not. A friend of mine likes to say, "God is greater than your heart." We can quickly dwell on feelings when we're overwhelmed or drowning. If you lose your job, worry can consume you. *How am I going to pay my bills? How am I going to keep up with the mortgage?* When your child is born with a disability, it's easy to fear the future. *How am I going to take care of him? What does this mean for the rest of my family?*

But God is greater than our hearts.

It's not that emotions won't get to us, or even get the best of us. Because when tough times come, we're going to get hurt and angry and upset. Think about it this way. Jesus had emotions, though He was always in control of them. They never got the best of Him. One time He walked into the temple and was horrified to see it had been turned into a flea market. It was a madhouse. People were buying and selling animals (just imagine the smell and the filth). Tables were laid out in every corner where businessmen exchanged currency with customers. It was like a zoo in the middle of a bank. Jesus was so angry. He drove everyone out of the temple, turned over the tables where financial transactions were taking place, and with a whip, ran out the sheep and cows. Yeah, Jesus was pretty upset.

What's my point? Feelings are normal. They can change on a dime. They come. And they go. We need to understand this and learn how to live above them, not by them. This means going deep, gaining knowledge about God by praying and reading His Word. Staying grounded in whose we are. And choosing to do what's right.

Listen, you're not always going to feel like doing the right thing. As a football player, I don't always feel like waking up early in the morning to train, but I have to do it. We're not always going to feel like being kind to a coworker who, frankly, is a jerk. We're not always going to feel like loving someone who is selfish and narcissistic. We're not always going to feel like zipping it when we really want to cuss someone out. We're not always going to feel like fighting for those who can't fight for themselves when we're going through problems of our own.

But the more you make the choice to live above your feelings, to trust

God instead of what you may feel like doing, the stronger your faith becomes. It's not about being perfect. We will always be on a journey of growing closer to God. I can tell you that I've messed up before and I'll mess up again. Chances are you will too.

Choose faith. Choose to trust God more than what you feel. Choose to believe in Him whether or not you feel like it. Like Chelsie, doing this especially when facing the giants in life is what can turn you into a mighty warrior.

An Unlikely Soldier

Two nations. Two armies. Ready for battle, primed to fight.

The first army stands in battle formation, swords and shields in hand. Positioned on one side of a mountain, they stare into a valley that separates them from their enemy, the nation whose land they want to conquer. The second army, thousands of troops lined up on the opposite side, is ready to defend the land with whatever it takes.

The first army has guts. Heart. They have a well-organized military campaign. But their weapons are second-rate.[11] That's just one disadvantage. There are more.

The second army, outfitted with seasoned soldiers, top-notch gear, and impressive artillery, stands tall and proud. Arrogance pulsing through their veins, they are confident. Though they don't make a move, they are sure of the outcome of battle. Victory for them. Oh, the sweet taste of victory. Besides their fierce iron weapons of war, they have a trump card, a secret advantage guaranteed to crush anyone who dares to oppose them.

Somewhere from the back line, a massive soldier appears. This special-forces, super monster machine towers over the entire army. He's covered in armor of bronze, making almost every inch of skin impenetrable, even for the most skilled knife-fighting combatant. We're talking about a dude bigger and badder than the giant Brad Pitt fights in the movie *Troy*.

When he emerges, he calls out in a deep-throated roar to the army on the other side of the valley, "Why do you come out to draw up in battle array? . . . Choose a man for yourselves and let him come down to me. If he is able to fight with me and kill me, then we will become your servants; but if I prevail against him and kill him, then you shall become our servants and serve us."[12]

No one is willing to stand up to him. So every day for forty days, this gigantic commando comes on the scene in front of his army to yell and threaten and demand an opponent from the other side. And day after day, no one accepts the challenge.

Until God's answer to the giant shows up.

He was a teenager, fifteen or sixteen. The youngest of eight boys in his family. A red-haired runt who looked after his father's flocks of sheep. Tending to them in green pastures, he was responsible for protecting them, keeping them from harm, and bringing them back home when ready. Oh, and he could also play a mean harp.

One day this boy's father tells him to take some food for his three brothers, who are soldiers in that first army, and for the leadership in command. "And bring back news of how they are doing, and how our army is looking."[13]

The boy nods and, at daybreak, rushes off. He finds his brothers in the battle line. They look worn, tired, defeated. And suddenly, a battle cry rings out in the valley. The soldiers assemble quickly into formation, weapons at their sides, eyes fixed. The boy peers through the mass of men in front of him, looks across the valley, and sees Rambo thundering his way through his fellow soldiers.

"Anyone today?" he roars. "Is there anyone brave enough to face me?"

Silence.

The boy elbows a soldier standing beside him and with his other hand points to the giant. "Who is this guy?" he asks, boldly. "And who on earth does he think he is?"[14]

The soldier gives the boy the rundown and then tells him that whoever ends up killing this bad dude not only gets the glory of accomplishing what looks like an impossible feat, but the king has also promised a reward in return, including a ton of money and his hot daughter in marriage.

Sounds like a good deal to me, thinks David.

Long story short, the little shepherd boy, skilled in instrument and song, goes before the king and tells him he's up for the challenge. I'll bet the king tries so hard not to laugh when this rosy-cheeked runt steps up. In his best trying-to-be-polite voice, he tells the kid to go home, but the boy is persistent, offering a litany of reasons why he's the man for the job. In caring for the sheep, he's had to fight and kill lions and bears with a club and his bare hands.

What is a king to do? He says okay.

The king gives the boy his own suit of armor, which looks absolutely ridiculous, like putting baby clothes on a G.I. Joe action figure. And the king's sword and shield? They're so heavy the boy can barely pick them up, let alone fight with them. "No thanks," he says, confidently. "I'm not used to all this stuff. I'll just use what I always use, my sling and my staff."

And off he goes. Stopping at a stream before heading to the front lines, the boy picks up five stones and puts them in his pocket. The perfect complement to his trusty sling. But why five stones? As confident as this kid was, was he afraid that he wouldn't kill the commando on the first, second, or even third try? No. He knew something. David knew Goliath had four family members, comparable contenders, just as big, strong, and dominating. If necessary, a stone for each bad boy. This kid had faith. He knew the kind of God he served. A big God. A God with whom big things are possible. And he trusted that God had his back no matter what.

An Unlikely Victory

Cut to the battlefield. When David steps out into the valley, his country's army cheering him on while simultaneously thinking he's a few sandwiches short of a picnic, Goliath stomps in front of his own army's front lines.

He looks at the kid with hatred, insulted by the obvious lack of competition. This is too easy. "Am I a dog, that you come to me with sticks?"[15] he thunders across the valley.

David is not moved by his opponent's intimidating appearance. He doesn't see that the odds are against him. He doesn't care that no one believes in him. He holds steadfast in his faith and replies to Goliath, "You come against me with sword and spear and javelin, but I come against you in the name of the LORD Almighty, the God of the armies of Israel, whom you have defied. This day the LORD will deliver you into my hands."[16]

He starts to sprint toward Rambo as the giant galumphs toward the boy, ready to crush the runt with one slam of his monstrous foot. With sling in one hand, stone in another, David picks up the pace. Both armies clank their spears and swords on their shields in a boisterous chorus that doesn't even match the roar that bellows out of Goliath's mouth.

And then, midstride, arms raised, David lifts the sling. Aim. Fire.

And while the second army gasps in horror, Goliath, blood gushing from the wound in the dead center of his forehead, collapses to the ground.

Game over.

But David has one last thing to do. He stands over Goliath, the giant's eyes open, frozen, and cuts off his head using Goliath's own sword.

Hooyah!

How does a shepherd believe he can crush a giant? Where does he get such confidence? Was it skill? A ton of practice? The power of positive thinking? I'm sure his skill set was part of it, but what gave David the courage was his deep faith. He lived it. While tasked with tending the sheep in the fields, he developed his relationship with God. And as a result of working his faith out, David was able to push aside his fears and crush every giant in his path—the lion, the bear, and Goliath.

Take It

I love what Jesus said in John 16:33: "Here on earth you will have many trials and sorrows. But take heart, because I have overcome the world" (NLT). What does it mean to take heart?

Don't give up. Be encouraged. Lift your spirits. And do this on purpose. With intention. Literally, *take* courage. Choose it. When you feel tired, discouraged, disappointed, or run down, make the choice to take heart.

Chelsie had to do this while fighting for her life. Do you think it was easy for her to take heart after getting so sick from dose after dose of chemotherapy? Do you think it was easy for her to take heart when all her friends were having a great time at college and she was stuck in a hospital? Do you think it was easy for her to take heart when the cancer came back with a vengeance? I'm sure it wasn't. But she did.

I'm not telling you something I don't have to do myself. I haven't always taken heart every day, but I'm trying to live this way. When I'm tired, when I'm feeling unsure, and when headlines and critics tell me I'll never make it, I try to choose courage time and time again to believe that God's got everything under control.

4

THE VOICES
OF NEGATIVITY

I like criticism. It makes you strong.

—LeBron James

When the plane touched down at the Morristown Airport in New Jersey, I had a glimpse of what was in store for the next year. The media circus had come to town.

Stepping down on the runway, the sun blinding, I saw a handful of people on the grass, waving wildly. Someone reached out to take me to a waiting car, at least from what I could tell from his arm movements. It was impossible to hear a word he was saying because of the two news-channel helicopters that were hovering low, cameras pointing down in my direction. Over a dozen reporters swarmed around, cameras clicking and tape recorders shooting my way as I made my exit from the airport. I was headed toward the New York Jets training facilities in Florham Park, just a few miles down the road.

It was March 2012. I had just been traded from the Broncos to the Jets as a backup quarterback to Mark Sanchez. Playing for New York, where just the name alone generates a mass of attention and big media spotlight, was like a double-edged sword. My agent repeatedly—and I mean repeatedly— told me to keep a low profile, to keep my head down. *Don't talk to reporters. Don't draw any attention your way. Just be a regular teammate.*

Got it.

And while I had no problem being one of the guys and staying out of the frenzy, New York takes media coverage to a whole new level. Would you expect any less from the Capital of the World?

I was told that the next day I had to give a televised press conference where I'd be introduced by the Jets. I had never before heard about any backup quarterback in sports history doing that. Talk about weird. And talk about getting exposure. I certainly didn't ask (nor would I have) for a press conference, but it was part of the job. I couldn't say no. Over two hundred members of the press showed up. In fact, there was so much media the conference had to be moved to the Jets' field house at the practice facility. All this to say, I wasn't quite sure how I was expected to lie low and stay out of the spotlight when it seemed others were pushing me toward it.

And that pretty much set the tone for my one-year stint as a Jet. That whole year, I tried hard to be one of the guys. I wanted to hang out with some of my teammates after games and chow down some burgers without it being reported in some paper that I ate dinner at this or that restaurant and with whom. It seemed everywhere I went, paparazzi followed. Cameras flashed in my face, reporters spit-fired questions, headlines blared—oh, I'll get there in a minute. And while my teammates were cool and I made some connections, it was tough. With all the media attention I received, it was almost impossible to be "one of the guys."

As far as being Sanchez's backup, contrary to what the media and some others may have said or portrayed, we weren't in a nasty rivalry. I wanted to be his friend and support him. I felt he wanted the same for me. While we tried, it wasn't necessarily the easiest thing in the world when some folks seemed to be pitting us against each other.

I wasn't angry because I wasn't a starting quarterback. I might have been disappointed, but I worked hard. I trained hard. I supported the team. I respected the leadership. And that whole year, I believed that eventually I was going to get my shot. I was reminded of what some of the coaches had told me repeatedly when I came on the team: "We are going to use your strengths, Timmy." "We are going to do this with you and that with you." It was exciting, knowing I was going to play. So at every practice and in every game, I did my best to be ready and waited for my chance. But the waiting only led to a chance that never came.

So yeah, about those headlines. While I was highly criticized in Denver— one reporter called me "the worst quarterback in the NFL,"[1] another said I was "the Kim Kardashian of sports,"[2] some called me inconsistent, others bashed me for my faith, and on and on—playing for the Broncos afforded me the opportunity to shut down my critics. I could prove them wrong. I could play my heart out and do my best on the field. I could use the game as an outlet to dial down those negative voices.

In the absence of playing time in New York, I didn't get that chance. I was probably more attuned to the negativity because of it. During that time I almost never watched TV or read blogs or browsed through social media, but I still couldn't help but hear or see the headlines, the tweets, the front covers. Whether I was driving into the city, buying a cup of coffee, or just talking to others, it was hard to miss. These stories seemed to find me everywhere I went.

One New York paper blared "God Help Him" on their front cover. Another, "Holy Smoked." One paper wrote that an anonymous teammate said I was "terrible." The stream of negativity was endless. While I tried hard not to let critics drag me down, it hurt coming from someone who was on my team, who was working with me to reach the same goal, who was fighting the same fight.

Then there was the commentator who seemed to make it his mission to take a succession of potshots—and I'm talking a lot. His words didn't necessarily shock me. What did, however, was the handwritten letter he sent, apologizing. This man wrote that one day his kids had asked him why he was bashing me so hard. This struck a nerve and he felt he needed to tell me he was sorry. Thus, the letter. His verbal rants stopped for a while. But then he shot right back out the gate in full force.

Hear my heart. I don't share all this for you to feel sorry for me. I don't need or want pity. And this is not a "Timmy Tebow woe is me" tirade. My point is you'll never silence the critics. I'm going to talk more about this later in this chapter, but for now understand that there will always be people in your life who will underestimate your potential, say that you'll never reach your dream or make that goal, or try to hold you back in some way. You may not be criticized in such a public manner, and some of the words you hear may sting a whole lot more than getting told you can't play football, but one day, if you haven't already, you will encounter a naysayer or two.

Here's the good news. What God knows about us is more important than what others think. In these moments, we need to go back to home base and remember whose we are. We need to remember that the God of the universe created us. We need to remember that we are His workmanship. That He has a purpose and a plan for our lives. And that He loves us unconditionally, no matter what. This doesn't mean He loves everything we do, of course. As Sinclair Ferguson wrote, "It is misleading to say that God accepts us the way we are. Rather he accepts us *despite the way we are.*"[3]

We were created by Love, in love, and for love. When we so much as catch a glimpse of how much God loves us, it changes how we think of our-

selves. We can withstand harsh criticism or hurtful words. We can be confident in who we are regardless of what others say.

My time in New York was pretty different than in Denver. As a Bronco,
I was the talk of the town. I had some good friends, a solid network of support. I lived in a beautiful gated community with basketball and tennis
courts. Oh sure, I had my share of critics, but for the most part, life was good.
I felt settled.

While playing for the Jets, I moved into a duplex in a quaint little New
Jersey town called Chatham. Not that I needed a ton of space, but it was
weird that my front door was only twelve feet away from the curb where
TMZ and other media were parked. Not to mention that I'd seen on six or
seven separate occasions strangers picking through my trash trying to find—
what? I have no idea. All this attention was happening way too close to where
I lived.

A Welcome Diversion

The spotlight in New York wasn't just for football. I was honored to receive a
ton of invitations to many cool events. For the sake of staying low, I couldn't
attend all of them, but the one I did go to was the Met Gala, the city's most
glamorous night in fashion. I didn't realize what a big deal it was at first. Hey,
I'm just a southern boy from Florida. But there I was, walking the red carpet,
rubbing shoulders with the likes of Julia Roberts and Jon Hamm. Movie
stars, famous musicians, and beautiful models were everywhere, all wearing
incredible, and some out of this world, fashion.

I was in the middle of an intense conversation with this really pretty girl,
when one of my agents tapped me on the shoulder. I may have pretended I
didn't feel her first few nudges, because I did not want to stop talking to this
girl.

"Hey, Timmy," she said, this time giving me a forceful elbow. "I want to introduce you to someone." *Okay, fine,* I pouted silently. I was not happy about keeping the pretty girl waiting.

"This is Alicia," my agent said, as a beautiful woman emerged from behind her.

I shook the woman's hand, noticing her magnetic smile, and said, "Hi, I'm Tim. It's so nice to meet you. I hope you have a great time tonight. God bless!" I was sincere, but that pretty girl was on my mind.

Right after Alicia walked away, my agent tapped me on the shoulder again, this time pretty hard.

"What?"

"Do you know who that was?" she asked, exasperated.

"Yeah, a lady named Alicia," I replied, wondering why she sounded a bit bent out of shape.

"That was Alicia Keyes, you big dummy! What's wrong with you?"

I just about kicked myself in the behind. I love Alicia Keyes, and my friend Bryan and I always talk about what a beautiful and incredible voice she has. Yeah, not one of my finer moments.

Outside of practices and games and going to that gala, I stayed in my duplex for the most part. Robby was with me. And while I was grateful for his company, we've never been the best at sharing emotions or feelings or any touchy-feely stuff with each other. And without many friends in town and not being involved in a church community, I was lonely. I'm sure a part of it was intentional. I did isolate myself as a way of not generating attention, but regardless, it was a pretty dark place.

In January 2013 the Jets hired Marty Mornhinweg as their new offensive coordinator. I was excited about his coming on board. *I might get a fresh start, a chance. This might be my shot, my time to show my potential. I'm ready! I'm going to prove everyone wrong!* For sure, I was optimistic.

I lasted two weeks into the off-season. Then, on April 29, 2013, I was released.

You already know what comes next. I was disappointed and, yeah, maybe even a little angry. I was also frustrated I wasn't cut earlier than I was. It would have been nice to have the time to get on another team. I was upset, but I also trusted that this was part of God's plan. It was a truth that I was having to remind myself of over and over.

And so, I left New York and once again focused on training to get in the best shape possible.

When It Matters

Criticism hurts. It's hard to hear harsh words from a journalist you might never meet in person. It's harder to hear the same from a trusted friend. It's important to note there are times we need to listen and pay attention to things others might say that we may not like. Not necessarily from talking heads or random people browsing through our Instagram accounts, but from those who know us best, like a spouse, a parent, a coach, a pastor.

For example, if a trusted mentor or friend advises you not to do something that might harm you down the road, your best bet is to listen without taking offense. Hard truth can sting, but it's better to deal with a bruised ego than a lifetime of regret. Besides, those who know us best may see our circumstances with more clarity than we do. We can all use some help with our blind spots. A close friend may notice warning signs of a potential relapse that we are oblivious to. Or a friend might see how our bad habits are negatively affecting those around us while we don't see it in the least. Proverbs 27:5–6 tells us, "Better is open rebuke than love that is concealed. Faithful are the wounds of a friend, but deceitful are the kisses of an enemy."

When people close to us challenge something we say or do, or think of saying or doing, it's important to understand their character. Ask yourself, *Are they coming from a place of sincerity and love? What are their intentions? Are they saying something that will benefit them in some way? Or are they truly looking out for my best interests?* It's about discernment, the ability to differentiate between who is supportive, loving, and telling you the truth—and who is not.

Sometimes hard truth needs to be told, whether we are doing the telling or someone else needs to tell us. While we may construe helpful advice or wise guidance as critical or negative, when it's offered in love and comes from a genuine place, it can change our lives for the better.

I call these talks courageous conversations.

Look, none of us wants to be judgmental. And nobody gets excited about having to tell a friend something that may initially hurt but might make the person better for it. I'm with you. I get it. I'm trying to get better about telling the truth in love. I've learned how important it is to affirm your love for a person before you bring the subject up, during the conversation, and when it's over. We must let our love for others be the reason they listen and the truth be the reason they change. (In the same vein, it will probably serve us well to listen to those who tell us hard things in this way.)

Now, let's get back to those naysayers, people who are critical and negative and who don't have a deep sense of love for you nor your best interests at heart.

SHUT IT DOWN

Even when you are grounded in who you are, it's not easy to hear others say bad things about, make fun of, or belittle you. It doesn't matter if you're an athlete, an entertainer, a teacher, a small-group leader, a high-school student, a business owner, or a stay-at-home mom, you will probably encounter folks, if you haven't already, who don't agree with your method of training, your leadership style, the way you dress, your business practices, or your child-rearing skills. And thanks to social media, we have millions of talking heads that each have something good or bad to say about anyone at any time.

Whether a Facebook troll tells you you're an idiot for wanting to write a book, or a neighbor mentions that you've put on a lot of weight, or a coworker bashes the project report you've poured your heart and soul into, or someone tries to discourage you from opening a restaurant because you'll probably fail, don't lose hope. Keep pressing on.

A promising star quarterback at an all-male boarding school had some big plans. He was athletic. Smart. Valuable. He had attracted attention from a ton of football programs around the country. Places like the University of Virginia, Virginia Tech, Vanderbilt, North Carolina, and Duke. Jacob knew what he wanted—to be in the NFL.

During a routine play in a scrimmage in August 2011, a defensive back crashed into Jacob's right knee, crushing it to the ground. The talented athlete blacked out. When he awoke, he noticed his knee protruding to the side. *Guess I'm out for the season,* he thought while moaning in pain. Jacob was taken to the hospital. A paramedic suggested it was probably a dislocation injury. Not great, but manageable. Something that would heal. And in due time, Jacob would likely be back running plays on the field.

What doctors discovered, however, was far worse. The main artery in Jacob's leg had been severed. Having developed compartment syndrome, a painful condition where swelling cuts off blood flow, which in turn causes muscles and nerves to die, Jacob's right leg had to be amputated just above the knee. The young man was stunned.

How on earth do you lose a leg playing football? I wondered.

After much physical rehabilitation, Jacob had to learn to walk using a prosthetic. And as he worked hard and got stronger, his desire to play football rekindled. It became something he wanted so badly. Not everyone thought he could do it. Jacob says that even "the doctors who I shared my goals with borderline laughed in my face. They told me it [playing football with one leg] had not been done before and that it was impossible. While it was discouraging to be shot down by professionals in the medical field, it also provided me with more passion and encouragement to prove those individuals wrong."

I met Jacob on Christmas Eve 2011 when I was playing for the Broncos. We've stayed in touch over the years. I've always admired Jacob for his fierce determination. He never let others stop him from dreaming big. He returned to play ball his senior year of high school, completing the season with 12 of 15 passes for 141 yards and three touchdowns.

Not everyone rooted for him. Jacob says, "During the season I also had critics and individuals who were not so encouraging. Some of that came from behind my back from individuals who were around me every day. For instance, some teachers at my high school." Still, Jacob pressed on, building his confidence and working toward his dream.

And then he got a call from Mike London, the football coach at the University of Virginia, who offered him a preferred walk-on position. Of course Jacob said yes. In his own words, "There is nothing sweeter than proving doubters and critics wrong."

The Negative Is Just Not Worth It

Criticism can at times be a bit painful for me to hear because I'm a people-pleaser by nature. I have almost no greater joy than honoring a coach or a father figure and doing my best to come through for that person. I love being able to do well alongside my teammates and crush it for them on the field. I want to strive to give my best, my all. I like making people happy, whether that means making wishes come true through my foundation, killing it in a game, or doing something extra-special for my mom for no reason. But I've learned that if I'm motivated only by making others happy, by their approval or praise, I end up with a hollow feeling.

While it makes you feel *good* to please people, it makes you feel *fulfilled* to please God.

There is nothing wrong with wanting to be the best, with wanting to succeed, with wanting to land that big deal, score that client, write that hit song, or dominate that game. It's good to have passion and work hard. However, it can become a problem when wanting the praise or the success or the pat on the back becomes everything. Why? Because it doesn't last! In 2007, after winning the Heisman, I was told I was the best in the world. And then three years later, I was told I couldn't throw.

Another thing. When you work so hard to make others like you and make them happy, the criticism you receive hurts even more. The wounds run deeper. The cuts are sharper.

It might surprise you to know that some of the deepest wounds I've experienced have come from fellow Christians. Unfortunately, I've seen too many believers playing a game instead of trying to love God and love people. The bottom line is that we as Christians, and even people who don't ascribe to faith, are not always going to agree on everything. Get into a deep conversation with someone—it doesn't matter how closely the person may share your beliefs, background, or worldview—and I'll bet any amount of money that one person is going to say something the other doesn't like or agree with. But I truly believe there is a way to disagree without being divisive or hostile.

I wonder what side of the equation you're on. Maybe you know too well the sharp cuts from negative words. Or the damage when someone spreads a false rumor about you. Or the painful verbal punches from bullies. Or the hurt that comes from being judged or looked down on. I know what it's like for a friend to not have your back. Negative words can hurt whenever it happens, but it's the worst when you don't see it coming.

And maybe, just maybe you've said something mean, condescending, judgmental, or negative to someone else. Maybe you're the one who said that snide remark, started that rumor, made that dig, or took that potshot. It is easy for me to remember times when others have hurt me with their criticism. It's harder to mention times I've hurt others with my words.

Several years back I distanced myself from one of my friends because he was involved with certain things I didn't support. Some of what I had said to him may have come across as judgmental, arrogant, or that I was better than he was. I still regret my choice of words.

We can intentionally or unintentionally hurt others for a bunch of different reasons. We might be jealous, ignorant from not having walked a mile in their shoes, or insecure.

I don't know why it seems we are better at tearing others down than lifting them up or cheering them on. This reminds me of a story I heard. Put a bunch of crabs in a shallow bucket and watch what happens. When a crab or two—the ones with the more adventurous personalities—attempt to climb out, the others who are below them will reach out and pull them back down. The bottom crabs will keep doing this so that no crab will ever escape.

Okay, so you and I are not crabs! But sometimes we share that same mentality: *If I can't have something—that great job, that perfect family, the dream come true, good health, an answer to prayer—neither can you.* Sometimes when we're facing adversity or hardship in our lives, we want everyone else to suffer with us. It's not fair that life moves on for others when our world is falling apart. And sometimes, people around us, even those closest to us, try to drag us down for whatever reason. And that hurts!

I don't know whether you are the one being criticized or you've done your share of criticizing. But I bet if we're honest, we've all had our share of both. Either way, we must make a conscious choice to avoid strife, jealousy, and division. We need to stop being deceived by the negative words others say against us. And we need to stop saying negative things about others. The criticizing, the name-calling, the complaining—none of this adds value, to others or to ourselves.

OUR WORST CRITICS

There's another critic who usually flies under the radar. You and me. Sometimes we are our own worst enemy. Consider what you've thought about yourself in the last week, or even in the last twenty-four hours, that has been negative.

I'll never finish this class.

My marriage sucks and it's my fault.

I'm too weak to beat this disease.

I'm not smart enough to fight for the promotion.

I could never go to that school or play that game or be on that team.

Why can't I be as (patient, kind, good looking, smart, successful, educated—fill in the blank) as that person?

So many times we are paralyzed from forward movement because we hold ourselves down. We compare our journeys, our losses, our victories, our marriages, our jobs, our dreams, our families with everyone else's. And in our minds, in some way, we fall short. We're never enough. That person has it easier. The grass is always greener. In our minds at least.

When our self-worth crumbles, when we're not feeling confident, when insecurities overwhelm us, we have to remember whose we are. It's pretty amazing how our identity lays the groundwork for everything! So remind yourself how much God loves you and that He has a unique purpose and plan for your life. And stop comparing yourself and your journey to someone else's.

Sometimes we can use these places of insecurity as a challenge, to help us dig deep into who we are and to grow. Instead of looking at someone else and feeling bad about yourself, how about looking at the areas in your life that you can improve? Maybe you need to work on your patience, self-control, or discipline.

Think about whether you want to wake up six months or a year from now being the same person you are today. Chances are, there are some things you could stand to change. We all can. Including me!

When I was younger, I was arrogant. And over the years I have grown a ton in the humility department. I'm also a perfectionist. I'm always striving to improve, working hard to be the best. This is not necessarily a bad thing, but I've found that my drive can sometimes blind me to my current blessings. I have to work on finding a balance between trying to be the best at whatever it is I'm doing and being thankful in the moment for what I have.

If there's something in your life you can stand to change, start working on making that happen. One step at a time. Look, I know there is no such thing as an easy fix. Our problems don't get solved overnight. Change takes time. But I also know it's important to live up to our potential. To be the person God created us to be.

Ask yourself, *Am I living just to get by? Or am I looking to improve, to change what I don't like about myself, to be a better person?*

I've been on many football teams. I've found there are two people who show up to practice: the person who wants to get better and the person looking to just get by. The first guy works hard, sweats, pours his energy into training, works on his agility, strength, and speed. The second guy basically just shows up. He's thinking about the movie he saw the night before and the girl he's going to go out with tomorrow. While the guy who just shows up might happen to be the best on the team, the fastest and the strongest, by not putting in the work, he might be wasting even more of his potential. And while that first guy might not be the best overall, he is doing all he can to be his personal best. That's what matters!

When I was a kid, my life changed when I realized that working out made me faster and stronger. This was my first experience learning about the power of change. I became pretty freakish about the human body and what it's capable of. I begged my parents for weight equipment, anything that would help me become a better athlete. And while Mom and Dad didn't have a ton of money, they provided what they could to encourage me to reach my goals. Dad even welded together equipment so I could weight train. It was creative and it worked! Knowing change was possible, I continued to work hard to optimize my fitness level.

I love the saying "Hard work beats talent when talent doesn't work as hard." Someone might be better, or stronger, or more talented, or more educated, but if we choose to put in the work of growth, we can perform at our best. And that's what matters.

Some people live by the principle "It is what it is." In other words, we are who we are. A zebra can't change its stripes nor a leopard its spots. I don't believe that idea when it comes to personal growth. I believe we can change. We can be better. We can become more self-controlled, more patient, kinder, more knowledgeable. We may have to seek outside help, take classes, read books, or pray a ton to get there, but we can change!

Every day is an opportunity to grow, to do something different, to be better. You might have failed yesterday. That's okay. It's more important to get back up. To try again. To keep at it.

Martin Luther wrote, "This life is not righteousness, but growth in righteousness. It is not healthy, but healing; not being, but becoming; not rest, but exercise. We are not yet what we shall be, but we are growing toward it. This is not the end, but it is the road."[4]

If you look at successful people, I'll bet at some point they all struggled with self-doubt or discouragement or were just down in the dumps. But they didn't stay in that place. They made the choice to keep believing, to keep pressing on, to keep growing and changing.

Growth is tough. It's painful. Do you know the only way to build muscle is to tear down the muscle fibers? This is what happens when you work out. And this process actually helps repair and strengthen the muscle.

Are you willing to grow spiritually? Emotionally? Are you willing to invest time, energy, and work into personal growth? Are you willing to stop complaining and to do something better to improve yourself? The best way to battle your inner critic is to grow, to change, to show progress in your areas of struggle.

As John Maxwell says, "Growth is the great separator of those who succeed long term from those who do not. When I see a person beginning to separate themselves from the pack, it's almost always due to personal growth."

GOD'S GOT IT

We must cease striving and trust God to provide what He thinks is best and in whatever time He chooses to make it available. But this kind of trusting doesn't come naturally. It's a spiritual crisis of the will in which we must choose to exercise faith.

—CHARLES SWINDOLL

was an Eagle. Well, not technically. Two years had passed since getting cut from the Jets. And despite being out of the NFL during that time, I was in the best shape of my life. And here I was, wearing the Philadelphia Eagles uniform, running plays and throwing passes during the preseason.

It was crazy how the invitation to be on the team came about. A few months earlier, in March 2015, I was in Boca Raton, Florida, exploring my next career steps. A lot of people around me were pressing me to shift gears. Offers were presented, some great, others entertaining, none ultimately the best. I took time to think about a few, deliberating the pros and cons. After all, for eighteen months, I hadn't gotten any calls to play as a quarterback.

As I started weighing these interesting options, Chip Kelly, the coach of the Philadelphia Eagles, called me. Would I consider playing for him? Um, yes, please! And the wheels started rolling to my becoming an Eagle. I was excited about working for Coach Kelly and thought the offense was perfect for me.

As I accepted the offer, I felt pumped. Surely God had paved the way to bring this about. *This is it. This is what I've been waiting for! I'm supposed to be an Eagle.* I gave God the proverbial high-five, imagining that though this next step was quite surprising given the timing, it was *the* moment I was destined for. I'll say I was ready. The training I'd done with Tom House and others during my hiatus after getting cut from the Patriots was paying off. Oh, and did I mention the first day of tryouts fell on March 16 (3/16)? Of course this was divine intervention!

I was stronger. Faster. Better. In fact, the team handed out awards during the off-season. I clinched the title for Big Skill, the prize a big, gaudy, WWE-esque belt (I still have it). My confidence was pretty high. *I'm ready. I'm going to be the best quarterback. And we're going to the Super Bowl.* If you don't know me by now, I like to dream big!

Getting another shot in the NFL was incredible. And it made me want to train even harder. As preseason opened, I was pumped. I had improved, showing glimpses during practices and games of my potential, signs that pointed toward what was possible.

With four quarterbacks on the team at this point, one would have to go. I was gunning for the highest position I could get. During this time, the media tagged along on our journey, trying to figure out who was going to get cut. I didn't pay much attention to the headlines or predictions. I just knew some would root for me and others would hope I'd fail. No matter, I strove hard to win.

It can be challenging to work hard and give the best performances you can while not getting obsessed with the guys you're playing, what squad you're on, how much time you're getting to play, what chances the coaches are giving you, and so on. After all, someone's got to go. And I hoped it wasn't me.

Right before we faced the New York Jets in our last preseason game, my phone blew up. My family and close friends called and texted with words of support. They prayed for me. They shared inspirational Bible stories. And they took me down memory lane, telling me some of their funniest memories of me playing football, which reminded me in a playful way of my love for the game. I remembered some of my loved ones reminding me to run free, uninhibited by the opinions of others.

I felt at peace. Content. I can honestly say I didn't have a feeling one way or the other of whether I'd get chosen for the team—and I was okay with that. I also was trying to seek what God wanted for my life. I was getting better at being more obedient to His guidance than gripping tightly to my plans and preferences. Obviously, I wanted to be the quarterback for the Eagles. I'd be lying if I said I didn't. But I also knew the reality. The coaches were forming a fifty-three-man team. Maybe I'd be on it. Maybe I wouldn't.

Though we lost to the Jets that night 18–24, I was getting into a better rhythm with the offense. I felt good about my performance. Actually I felt really good. I threw two touchdown passes and had thirty-two rushing yards on four carries against the Jets. It wasn't the best, but it was good.

After I finished up with the press after the game, one of the members of the Eagles public-relations team came up to me and said, "Dude, great job! I don't think you have anything to worry about."

I smiled, grateful for the kind words but still cautious. Considering the letdown with the Patriots two years earlier, and the Jets before that (more on New York in the next chapter), I tried to guard my heart, reminding myself that I wasn't in control; God was. And it wasn't my job to orchestrate or prompt or change His plan.

For hours, my phone buzzed constantly with calls and texts from family, friends, and even acquaintances.

"Awesome game, Timmy!"

"You nailed it, buddy!"

"Proud of you!" One of my agents called and said, "Great job, Timmy. I'm really feeling good about this!"

Sometime that night, one of the assistant coaches approached me, hinting I'd be in Philadelphia for a long time. "Hey, Timmy," he said. "Have you bought a house yet? Where are you planning to live?"

Good signs, you'd think. At least more signs than not that pointed toward staying on board.

Before I left the stadium to head back to my hotel, I asked someone on the staff whether or not I should come in the next day. I was scheduled to fly out to Scottsdale, Arizona, in the morning but had no problem postponing the trip for a day or so if necessary. Besides, if I were going to get cut, I wanted to be around to hear the news. The drama of getting released was getting old. I don't remember who it was, but someone told me, "Sure, Timmy. Why don't you come back, just in case."

So I did. On Friday, the morning after the last preseason game, I headed to the NovaCare Complex.

Déjà vu.

I trained. I showered. And I did all these things slowly, as drawn out as humanly possible. I wanted to give the powers-that-be every opportunity to find me if needed. I waited. And waited. And waited.

Nothing.

Erik texted me during this time: "Are you doing alright? I know you have peace, but I also know waiting isn't that much fun. ☺ 'It is God who arms me with strength and keeps my way secure' (Psalm 18:32 NIV)."

"I'm doing real good," I replied. "God's got it."

I was on a plane headed to Scottsdale just before 4:00 p.m. that day, exactly twenty-four hours before the Eagles' deadline to secure their roster. A flight attendant had just started to introduce herself and the captain, welcoming all passengers on board, when my phone lit up.

"Matt Barkley traded to Arizona Cardinals" blared an ESPN headline.

What? One of the quarterbacks I was competing against was taken out of the equation. I was pretty taken aback, but for the most part I was calm. Collected. I had to be.

The news of the trade flooded that airplane space pretty quickly. The flight attendant who had just begun her spiel of "Please make sure your seat backs and tray tables are in their full upright position" turned to me with a smile and said, "Congratulations, Tim!" Others around her in the first-class cabin followed suit. Some of the passengers high-fived me, offering congratulations. Even the pilot popped his head in to see me. As hundreds of texts poured in at the news of the Barkley trade, all saying some form of congratulations, it felt pretty overwhelming.

While in the past years, this hoopla would have been a high, at the time I felt more in tune, more at peace with whatever would happen. I was optimistic, but I didn't ride the wave of assuming I was an Eagle.

At this point in time, so many things had happened that were leading me to believe this was it, that this was the plan. That I was meant to be an Eagle. The news of the Barkley trade seemed to be the clincher. By the time I touched down on the Arizona tarmac, no one from the Eagles had reached out to tell me I was cut. And throughout the rest of that day and night, I received text after text from teammates telling me congratulations. I slept really well that night.

At 10:00 a.m. Saturday morning, my phone rang.

It was Coach Kelly. *Sigh.*

I couldn't sit still for this conversation. I opened the door of my hotel room and started pacing the hallway as we talked. "We made the decision to let you go, Tim," Coach told me, as I took slow, deliberate steps down the carpeted floor of the Fairmont Princess hotel. "I think you need more reps," he continued.

Disappointment set in, frustration. A flashback of practices and games raced through my mind.

Didn't he see how much better I got? How much I improved? Didn't he see what happened, the touchdowns I scored, after I got my hands on the ball?

And as I walked slowly back into my room and sat, rigid, on the edge of the hotel bed, I stared at the floor. My plan broken. My dream jerked back again. As peaceful as I had felt before this phone call, as much as I knew that God was still in control, I was hurt. Torn.

Did this really happen? Again?

Almost immediately after the call ended, sportswriter Adam Schefter broke the news on Twitter: "Eagles release QB Tim Tebow, per source."

I quickly arranged a circle-of-trust conference call. I was grateful for the support and encouragement my loved ones offered. I felt a strange mix of emotions. For the record, I wasn't happy. I was disappointed. Partly in disbelief. But as hard as it was, fighting against my natural feeling to stay upset, I forced myself into the space of contentment. I chose to return to the state I was in before I was released, the place of peace, when I held on to my faith that God was in control, no matter what happened. Though I wasn't thrilled with the outcome, I made the choice, yet again, to believe that God really, really, really had this. It wasn't easy, but I'll say the letdown wasn't as painful as being let go from the Patriots.

Later that day, Coach Kelly held a press conference where he broadcast his decision. In his words, "We felt Tim has progressed, but we didn't feel he was good enough to be the [No.] 3 right now."[1]

Later that afternoon, still making the choice to trust God, I tweeted,

"Thanks @Eagles and Coach Kelly for giving me the opportunity to play the game I love! Romans 8:28 #Blessed."

Was I blessed? Yes. Did I necessarily believe it with every pore in my being? I was trying. I really, really was. I made the choice—and kept making it—to trust God.

GOT DOUBT?

"I thought God had planned this."

"I thought He was the One who opened the door for me!"

"How could He have given me something only to take it away?"

"Why is this taking so long?"

When life doesn't turn out exactly as we wanted or had planned even after praying and feeling pretty sure about God's directions, the questions come (like the ones above). A lot of them. And fast. You may know exactly what I'm talking about.

It's what happens when you finally get the job after fifteen dead-end interviews and then get let go three months later.

It's what happens when, after you worked so hard on your presentation, an executive at the table turns down the deal.

It's what happens after your spouse tells you she's leaving.

When life throws us curve balls, some devastating, it's easy to allow doubt to creep in, no matter how strong of a Christian we think we are. *Why me? Why now? Why?* We doubt ourselves. We doubt God's plan. And oftentimes, we doubt God. Why would He do something, or allow something to happen, that breaks our hearts?

Hey, I've doubted. I've asked many a time, *God, where are You? I was depending on You. I thought You had this?* Sometimes I wonder if I wanted something so bad that I took the reins to make it happen, only to fall flat on my face.

I can't tell you why bad things happen or why our dreams and plans shatter. It's an age-old question that people have asked for centuries and will continue to try to answer, debate, and write books about. This is something Job talked about in the Bible, struggled with. Though most of us haven't gone through the intense level of suffering he had, most of us can relate to his questions, to his struggle with wanting to know why God would orchestrate tragedy.

Job is a righteous dude. He doesn't just go to church and go through the motions. He truly loves God. He is generous, kind, and faithful, the kind of guy you want to hang out with and even be like. He is wealthy, the richest guy in the neighborhood, in fact, but he's not smug about it. He's a humble guy, talks the talk and walks the walk.

One ordinary day, out of the blue, God and the devil have an interesting conversation about Job.

God is the epitome of a proud papa, beaming from ear to ear about His beloved child. "Have you noticed my friend Job? There's no one quite like him—honest and true to his word, totally devoted to God and hating evil."[2] Job definitely gets the proverbial pat on the back.

The devil rolls his eyes. "Gimme a break. The only reason Job is so faithful is because You give him everything. Who wouldn't sing Your praises if they had a huge house, a great job, and a wonderful family? The guy has it so easy!"[3]

After a dramatic pause, nodding in thought, the devil continues, sharing a bold idea. "Take it all away," he challenges God. "Take away everything remotely good in Job's life. Then see what happens."[4] The bet seems an easy win.

Thing is, God knows this is not a bet. This is the story of one man's life. A man who loves God and whom God loves. In His omniscience, God knew the end result. This story was planned beforehand. Essentially, God played the devil into His own hands.

In a series of devastating tragedies, Job loses everything. His financial assets get wiped away. His estate is literally crushed by natural disasters. His children die. He gets sick; painful boils cover every inch of his body. Job is heartbroken, in pain, and barely hanging on emotionally. His friends visit, and though Job is hoping for an encouraging word or two, instead they try to figure out why their buddy is suffering so much.

"You must have done something evil," they offer, their words peppered with judgment, self-righteousness. "It has to be your fault." (Hmm, it's so easy to point blame or give your two cents when you're not walking in someone else's shoes, isn't it?) Needless to say, these words don't help.

Job's wife isn't any better in the encouragement department. "Oh for Pete's sake," she groans, throwing her hands up in despair. "Just curse God and die already."[5] In other words, give up. Call it a day. (Note to self: don't marry a woman like this.)

But Job doesn't turn his back on God. He does, however, wrestle with doubt. He prays. He questions. *Why, God, why?* I love what he says at one point. "Though He slay me, I will hope in Him. Nevertheless I will argue my ways before Him."[6] *Even though my world is shaken, and even though I will ask why, I'm still going to trust You. I'm still going to put my hope in You.* Wow! I admit I'm not sure I would have the guts to say that first part if I went through what Job did.

In response to Job's queries, God doesn't give him a list of reasons why he had to go through so much, nor does He show him the purpose in the plan. Instead, He turns the whole thing around and throws some questions Job's way. "You ask me all these things, son. Well, it's your turn. I've got some questions for you." And in a beautiful monologue that illustrates His power, creative ability, and omniscience, God asks Job, "Where were you when I laid the foundations of the earth? Have you seen where darkness dwells and the way that leads to light? Do you know the path of the stars above? The workings of wisdom?"[7] On and on God questions Job with things so deep, the guy wouldn't even begin to know how to answer them.

It's important to note that God isn't shaming Job. He is telling him that there is purpose and meaning to everything He does. And though we may or may not know it in this life, there is a plan. We can doubt. We can question. We can wonder. But there always is a purpose.

Eventually Job's trials end, and God restores to Job even more than what he had before.

Why do bad things happen to us? Here's what I know: we are broken people living in a fallen world. And because of our sin nature and free will, our freedom to make choices, our world bubbles over with addiction, illness, betrayal, crime, heartache, disappointment. Suffering exists. Remember Jesus's words to always "take courage" or "take heart"? Why did He say this? Because "here on earth you will have many trials and sorrows."[8] He was warning us that this life isn't going to be a cakewalk. And there will be times when it gets really, really hard.

And imagine if there were no God. Instead of there being a purpose in the pain, pain would be meaningless. There would be no hope. All the evil people who have committed atrocities just get away scot-free. There's no justice without God. No forgiveness and no redemption. Evil ultimately wins.

When we ask questions, when we doubt, when we wonder if God is going to pull through, or wonder why He didn't pull through, or wonder why our miracle is taking so long, or why the miracle never came at all, remember that doubt is normal. God isn't scared of your questions. Bring them to Him. It's better to vent to Him than to run from Him. But just like I've talked about earlier, just like we have to strive to live above our feelings, we must strive to live above our doubts, above our questions.

I don't know what you're going through right now. Maybe your health is failing, your marriage is falling apart, your addiction is rearing its ugly head, or you feel overwhelmed by anxiety or depression. Know that your questions, your whys, may be answered on this side of heaven, or they may not be. But don't let that stop you from fighting the good fight and keeping the faith. Don't let it stop you from trusting in His plan for your life. God will come through in some way or another. Sometimes in the form of an answer to prayer, other times in the form of comfort, peace, and perspective far above what's possible in our human strength.

A HEART FOR ANOTHER

In December 2012, sixteen-year-old Garrett Leopold was in a Florida hospital, waiting for a heart. It would be his third one. And without it, he would die.

Garrett appeared healthy when he was born, a hefty nine-plus-pounder. Then, in less than twenty-four hours, his vitals started to fail. Right before being helicoptered to Shands Hospital at the University of Florida, a nurse asked his parents if she could pray with them for Garrett, who was now covered in a mesh of wires and fighting for his tiny life.

At Shands he was diagnosed with hypoplastic left heart syndrome. Unknown at the time, while he was in his mother's womb, his left ventricle had stopped growing. Without another heart, Garrett wouldn't survive.

Susan, Garrett's mom, said, "We could only pray for God's will. This was obvious to us when we stopped in mid-prayer, realizing that to pray for a heart transplant for our son was asking for another child's life to end." Garrett was only twelve weeks old when he underwent his first heart-transplant surgery. Though the next few years consisted of countless doctor appointments, medications, and checkups, Garrett was relatively healthy.

After spending his first two weeks in kindergarten, he nonchalantly told his mother he felt full and showed her his unusually swollen belly. Garrett hadn't eaten too much; he was diagnosed with Burkitt's lymphoma, a rare form of cancer that sometimes develops after heart transplants. After four months of chemotherapy, including a three-month hospital stay, the cancer was gone. Since that time, however, Garrett has had to visit the hospital every two months for intravenous infusions that doctors hoped would boost his immune system.

In June 2012, Garrett had a heart biopsy. Bad news. He was diagnosed with coronary artery disease. And he needed another heart.

I met Garrett for the first time while playing college ball. A friend had invited him to come into the locker room after the 2006 National Championship celebration to meet some of the players. He was such a sweet kid, shy but full of life. I don't remember exactly when, but I do remember spending some time with Garrett at Shands Hospital before we granted him a W15H in August 2012, when his health was deteriorating. I was playing for the New York Jets at the time. The foundation flew him and his family out to see our preseason game against the Philadelphia Eagles.

Less than a month later, Garrett was admitted to the pediatric ward at Shands, where he was immediately put on the heart-transplant list. My friend stayed there for six months connected to an IV and heart monitor. And he waited.

When the first week of March 2013 rolled around, Garrett's condition took a turn for the worse. His heart started beating in an irregular rhythm.

With the outlook grim, on Friday evening, March 8, Garrett's parents got a call from the hospital. Come quick, they were told, you need to be here for your son.

Early Monday morning, at 3:23 a.m., a donor heart became available. Garrett's mom and his dad, Erich, remember the text they got from the doctor. "The heart is here. The transplant has started."[9]

Garrett's parents were ecstatic at the news but also felt heartbroken for the donor who lost his or her life. Susan said, "We never can say 'thank you' enough for such a gift."[10]

On Monday, Garrett had a new heart.

Though most organ donors are anonymous, it didn't take too long before both families began to realize a connection, both heartbreaking and life changing. Eighteen-year-old Amanda Pierce was a senior in high school, making plans to begin her studies at a community college and then transfer to Florida State University. She wanted to be a special-education teacher. On Friday night, March 8, at the same time Garrett started fighting for his life, Amanda was driving to Tallahassee. There was an accident in front of her. She swerved her car trying to avoid it and hit a tree instead. Amanda was pronounced dead early Saturday morning, her heart a perfect match for Garrett.

Amanda's family found Garrett through social media. When they reached out initially, Garrett wasn't ready to connect. He struggled with survivor's guilt, knowing a price was paid for his life.

Finally, on March 9, exactly one year after Amanda passed away, Garrett and his mom met face to face the family of the girl who saved his life. He brought with him a stethoscope so Amanda's mother could hear her daughter's beating heart.

In a powerful and emotional meeting, Amanda's father showed Garrett and his mom pictures of their beloved daughter. And with her eyes closed, the stethoscope in her ears, Amanda's mother Laurie placed the instrument on Garrett's chest. As she listened to her daughter's heartbeat, with tears rolling down her face, she whispered in a broken voice the words "I love you."[11]

Later, in an interview with local media, Laurie said something I'll never forget: "There is no doubt in my mind that God intervened. This is tragic and awful and unspeakable, but it can at least still bring something miraculous from the tragedy."

Garrett recently said, "Amanda's parents are loving and always tell me I am worthy of Amanda's heart. We have met many times for dinner, concerts. Amanda's family is a part of my family. I am a junior at Mulberry High School, and some days are rough and some days are better. I feel really humbled and honored, also blessed, to say I received the gift of life though Amanda's heart. God has been good."

Not every prayer is answered in the way that we want. Sometimes things happen for reasons we can't explain, that don't make sense, that seem unfair. If today you're going through a tough time, know that it's for a purpose. One of my favorite quotes is from my big sister Christy. In the midst of her struggles with health and the challenges of being a missionary overseas, she became convinced, "God will never waste pain that's offered to Him." I love that. God will never waste your pain. He will never waste your heartache. He will never waste your loss.

If you've lost something precious to you—a dream, a marriage, a child—I can't tell you exactly the purpose or plan, or what the future holds, but I will say that He is loving, He is sovereign, and that although your heart may be broken in a million pieces, He will never leave or forsake you.[12] And He can and will use even the bad to orchestrate good.

I want to be clear that I'm talking about pain that's given to Him. If we hold on to our hurts, our heartaches, our struggles, our losses and refuse to surrender them to Him, we become bitter. And we relinquish the opportunity for God to do something with it—whether it's to mold our character, teach us something important, grow us in some way, or make a difference in the lives of others.

The Bible tells us, "God causes all things to work together for good to those who love God, to those who are called according to *His* purpose."[13] If we let Him, God can use all things for good, even the bad.

Surrendering our suffering, our disappointments, our regrets, our sadness to God isn't something that's easy. It doesn't necessarily come naturally to us. And it's usually not something we want to do. Let me put it this way: surrender in this way is simply saying something like "Look, God, I'm really struggling right now. And I'm asking for help. Please work this out in some way, somehow, for good."

I know it's easier to hold on to the bad stuff, to control it to some extent, and to keep God out of the picture. But when we do, we're the ones that suffer. Another thing we need to remember is that God has designed a huge and masterful plan. Something beyond ourselves. A missionary named Paul said it this way: "Now we see in a mirror dimly, but then face to face; now I know in part, but then I will know fully."[14]

God's perspective is bigger than ours. He is more knowledgeable than we are. He sees beyond today and even tomorrow. As I've said before, what kind of God would He be if we could figure out everything about Him?

Trust God. Trust His heart. Trust that He loves you. Trust that He has a plan. If you have to do this grudgingly at first, dragging your feet along the way, that's okay. It's at least one step in the right direction.

BITTERNESS AND TRUST CANNOT COEXIST

It may not be easy for you right now to fully trust God with your heart or your circumstances. There are times I struggle to believe that He's got everything already worked out and that I just need to simply believe. Trusting God doesn't mean you have to be excited about the trials you're going through; it just means choosing to trust, saying yes to Him, rather than turning your back and calling the whole faith thing off.

Just like fear is a powerful emotion that gets in the way of believing in God, so is bitterness. And it's an easy thing to feel. Who wouldn't be bitter when, through no fault of your own, you lost your job, went bankrupt, and didn't know how you were going to house and feed your kids? Who wouldn't be bitter if your sister was in a car accident and didn't make it but the drunk driver who crashed into her did? Though the temptation to drown in resentment may be great, all bitterness does is eat away at us like a disease.

Christian apologist Lee Strobel says, "Acrid bitterness inevitably seeps into the lives of people who harbor grudges and suppress anger, and bitterness is always a poison. It keeps your pain alive instead of letting you deal with it and get beyond it."[15] Put more bluntly, "Bitterness is like drinking poison and waiting for the other person to die."[16]

While we can choose to trust God and still wrestle with doubt, we cannot trust Him while holding on to bitterness. Bitterness and trust cannot coexist.

Gary Albers remembers being in vacation Bible school as a kid. Whenever the teacher led the class in singing the classic tune "Jesus Loves Me," Gary would sometimes follow the teacher's lead and numbly sing along. Other times he wasn't able to even stomach mouthing the words. When he heard the phrase "Jesus loves the little children, all the children of the world" in another song, his heart would ache.

Jesus must have forgotten about us Albers kids, he thought.

Gary's childhood was dark, painful. He and his siblings experienced things no child should ever have to endure. After finding out her husband had molested one of their own daughters, Gary's mother kicked his dad out of the house. To survive financially, she rented out her basement to a tenant who sexually molested Gary.

Over the course of time, Gary's mother remarried five times. Three of her husbands were violent alcoholics. Some were sexually and physically abusive. One of them even put Gary in the hospital after Gary walked in on him molesting one of his sisters. He beat Gary badly, breaking his nose and ribs and even tearing the tissue around the boy's heart.

Feeding a growing rage, Gary knew it was time to fight back. He started studying martial arts, learning how to fight effectively. It wasn't a hobby. It was about survival. And ultimately his martial-arts training betrayed him.

Gary became a fighter. With a deep-rooted hatred for men because of what they had done to his sisters, Gary, well into adulthood, picked fights with people he knew and ones he didn't. Sometimes he had a reason that seemed a good excuse at the time, like beating a violent and abusive stepfather within an inch of his life. Other times it was a way of releasing his rage. He rarely lost.

Gary's hard reputation and fighter instincts got him into trouble in the military when he knocked out a shore-patrol officer who was trying to apprehend Gary for fighting. This resulted in a disciplinary hearing.

The bitterness grew, year after year, hardening Gary's heart. Although there were times he'd justify a fight, he had a sense he was turning into a monster. Gary's traumatic past and the growing rage had such a hold on him, it was beginning to define his present and his future. But he couldn't let it go.

Though he had become a Christian after getting out of the military, Gary admits to going through the motions. It's important to note that just because you ask Jesus to come into your life and forgive you for what you've done wrong, it doesn't mean you won't do wrong again. You don't instantly become this perfect person, and all the bad things you struggle with don't immediately go away. While we are justified through faith in Jesus, God still has to transform us from the inside out. And that takes time.

Although Gary knew Jesus and as a result his life produced some good fruit, it didn't mean he didn't have any rotten apples as well. Gary struggled to get over the abuse he had experienced and witnessed as a kid. He was angry, full of rage, and suffered from frequent nightmares. At one point, he even contemplated committing suicide.

But then, God broke him. In a good way. Gary began to realize that he couldn't fully trust in God and continue to be bitter about his past. It was time to let go. It was time to surrender, fully. And when he made a conscious choice to commit to his faith, to begin to learn what it means to trust God, his life changed. He began to experience freedom. The darkness in Gary's heart was gone. He felt, for the first time in his life, peace. And he had no desire whatsoever to punch the living daylights out of anybody.

Gary says, "Jesus took everything I went through to the cross—the abandonment, the abuse, the beatings, the disappointment, the shame . . . and He brought me up from a horrible pit." Psalm 40 holds a special place in his heart.

I waited patiently for the LORD;
And He inclined to me and heard my cry.
He brought me up out of the pit of destruction, out of the
    miry clay,
And He set my feet upon a rock making my footsteps firm.
He put a new song in my mouth, a song of praise to our
    God. . . .

How blessed is the man who has made the LORD his trust.
    (verses 1–4)

Gary is the proud father of three wonderful adult children. His son Kevin was deeply impacted by his father's journey. He says, "Watching my dad's inner transformation was beyond inspiring. It influenced me and the way I want to live and be a father to my children. What my dad went through as a child wasn't in vain. God used that terrible experience to turn him into the amazing man, husband, father, and grandfather he is today."

God didn't waste Gary's pain. And He won't waste yours. You never know how the tough times you are going through today will inspire someone else tomorrow.

THE OTHERS

I would rather walk with a friend in the dark
than walk alone in the light.

—HELEN KELLER

Getting to the remote village wasn't easy. It was an adventure—scaling rocky terrain, getting scraped by prickly bushes, swatting away the gigantic mosquitoes. Definitely not for the faint of heart. But whoever said my first mission trip to the Philippines was supposed to be easy?

I was fifteen years old, excited to do great things on the other side of the world. With Dad leading the charge, a group of us visited local hospitals, prisons, marketplaces, orphanages, and schools, sharing God's love with anyone we met. I had an awesome time meeting the men, women, and children of this beautiful country and was blessed to love on them. And I'll never forget that one remote village we visited that took us a good part of the day to reach.

We rode for a while in a rugged Jeep, bouncing in our seats on a steep and rocky dirt path. When the road stopped, we got out and finished our journey on foot. Our first order of business was climbing a mountain. Seriously, a mountain. And I'm not talking a dinky little hill. We spent hours hiking a beaten and rocky path surrounded by tropical trees, some sky high. I felt like Indiana Jones, trekking through the wilderness trying to find the Holy Grail. Sweat poured down my back, partly from the strenuous climb and partly from the scorching sun that made the already sweltering day feel a hundred degrees hotter. But it was just a part of the adventure. And I loved it!

By the time we reached the top, the view was incredible. A blanket colored by more shades of green than I'd ever seen in my life stretched out before my eyes. Well, since I'm technically color blind, I'm pretty sure it was green, since I was looking at trees. Clouds dotted the blue sky so close it was as if I could reach out and touch them. Beautiful.

When we stepped into the town, the villagers immediately surrounded us, their eyes wide with curiosity. Most of them had never left the island or owned a television, so for many that day it was their first time seeing Americans. The Filipinos were especially curious about the girls in our group who had blond hair. They were so intrigued by the light color, they would reach out and pat them on their heads. Some even twirled pieces of their hair around their brown-skinned fingers.

As our group walked through the village, men, women, and children followed. Some of the adults kept their distance but never took their eyes off of us. The children couldn't come close enough. They bounced around us, laughing and chatting away in their native language as if we were old friends. Some wore shirts and pants that were ripped, stained. Others didn't have shoes on. These kids didn't have much materially speaking, but they were happy. You could see it on their faces.

With the help of the some of the locals, we started gathering the people together for a meeting at the high school. "We have news to share with you," we said, "good news."

The tiny town shut down. People working, cooking, cleaning, or playing stopped what they were doing and took off to follow us, to hear what we had to say.

At least twelve hundred people gathered right outside the high school, packed like sardines around the makeshift platform. Some stood, others squatted. All listened to our message of hope. That afternoon, it was my turn to speak, with the assistance of a translator. The people in the first row sat on the ground right at the tip of my boots. And if I leaned over just a foot or so, I could touch row seven.

Right before I started sharing, something caught my attention. From the corner of my eye, I noticed three boys moving, slowly, from one side to the other, around the back edge of the crowd. They were far away, but as I began to talk to the crowd, I noticed they would take a few steps in sync, stop and turn their heads to listen to what I was saying, move a few feet more, and stop again. It looked like they were hoping no one would notice. Then, they cut behind a building and were gone.

I was stunned. It seemed all the people in the village had not just paused their day to come and hear our message; they also wanted to get as close to us Americans as physically possible. So why did these three kids leave? And, I wondered, why did I notice? The crowd was so big I could have easily missed them. It seemed I was drawn to them.

As I talked about the love of God and the special plan He has for each of us, I couldn't get those three boys off my mind. *I have to find them. I have to talk to them.* I gave an invitation for whoever wanted to ask Jesus into their hearts, prayed with the folks who raised their hands, and then closed the meeting, thanking everyone for allowing us to be there and share with them. While walking away from the makeshift platform, mobbed on every side, I said, "God bless you," and gave as many hugs as I possibly could, scanning the area left and right, hoping to catch a glimpse of those three kids.

As I turned the corner behind the school building, I noticed a bamboo hut. Then, a head with a mop of dark hair peered out of an opening. A boy walked out of the hut, smiling. *Score!* He was one of the three.

I waved and said, "Hi there! I'm Timmy!" with a big smile on my face, inviting him to come toward me. He didn't say a word in reply but started walking my way. When he was close enough, he reached out his little hand. Wrapping his fingers around two of mine, he led me toward the bamboo hut where, I imagined, his two buddies were. Although I was a total stranger, he seemed comfortable around me, like I was a friend. And I couldn't help but see something special in him.

I crawled inside, hands and knees brushing the earth, and noticed the one boy lying down on a cot. The other sat beside him with his legs crossed, his hand caressing his friend's arm in a comforting manner. The boy who brought me in sat down on the opposite side of the one lying down, his hand on his friend's shoulder. They were smiling but nobody said a word. Just three pair of eyes staring at me.

Still on my knees, I looked over to the boy stretched out on the cot and introduced myself. I was going to ask if they wanted to shoot some hoops or something. When I took my eyes off the boy's face, I noticed why he was lying down. His legs were on backwards.

My heart fell. Fighting back tears, I felt small in that moment. I wanted to help him, to do something. I was touched by the body language of the other two boys, who never took their hands off him. It was a protective and tender gesture.

I asked them their names, how old they were, and other things. Finally, the quiet spell broke. They rattled off answers in broken English, animated. After a few minutes I said, "I saw you guys while I was speaking. Why did you leave?"

Sherwin, the boy on the cot, answered. "Our school principal wanted to impress the Americans." He paused, looking down at his legs. As his eyes filled with sadness, he said, almost in a whisper, "And the principal said that I'm not very impressive."

My heart broke more. This boy should have been the first one seated in the first row. This boy should be loved, encouraged, lifted up—not dismissed, ignored, or discarded like he wasn't good enough. In spending a few precious minutes with these three boys, I shared with them the love of Jesus. I told them that God had a special plan for them. I thanked the two boys for being awesome friends and told Sherwin that God created him perfect and that God thought he was very, very impressive.

Suddenly, I heard commotion outside the hut. My team was preparing to leave and was looking for me.

"I'm sorry," I said to Sherwin and his friends. "I have to go."

"Can you at least carry me out?" Sherwin asked.

"Of course!" I picked the boy up and motioned for his friends to follow. They walked on either side of me, one holding Sherwin's hand, the other his backward foot. Together we headed toward where our team had gathered and was preparing to leave. What's interesting is that in noticing all the "Americans" lavishing special attention on Sherwin, suddenly the people who didn't think much of him were acting super nice, like that principal, who appeared out of nowhere.

And then, just before we said good-bye, the boys told me they wanted to trust Jesus and invite Him into their hearts. It was a beautiful moment, three friends who together accepted the gospel of hope.

I looked at Sherwin before handing him over to his two pals. All four of us had tears in our eyes. "I can't wait to see you in heaven, buddy," I told him, tousling his thick dark hair with my hand.

He looked at me with a wry smile, his eyes sparkling. "Timmy, I can't wait to run with you in heaven."

In that moment, something struck a chord in my fifteen-year-old heart.

I realized after meeting Sherwin that while I wanted to be the best quarterback in the world, I also wanted to impact lives. I wanted to bring faith, hope, and love to those needing a brighter day in their darkest hour of need. I wanted to fight for those who couldn't fight for themselves. I wanted to fight for Sherwin. I wanted to fight for people like him. And as I stood on top of that mountain, surrounded by a sea of beautiful Filipinos, the vision for our foundation began. Inspired by these boys, I envisioned someone holding the hand of a hurting child, and another getting help to fill the need. For this is what Sherwin's two friends did. One stayed behind to comfort him, and the other, it seemed, went on his way to look for me.

The Best Kind of Friend

Not that I'm comparing myself to Michael Jordan, but stay with me for a minute. Imagine being in middle school. And imagine being a diehard Michael Jordan fan (this might come easy for some of you). Say he was coming to your school to host a slam-dunk competition. Can you imagine having to stay back with your friend who just broke his leg? Would you be so quick to say "no thanks" to this once-in-a-lifetime opportunity, something so fun and so incredible that you'll probably never get to do it ever again in your life just because your friend couldn't go? Don't hate me for this, but in my younger years, I would have likely left my friend in a heartbeat. "I hope you feel better, but I gotta go and meet Michael Jordan! God bless you, buddy!"

But not these two friends of Sherwin.

Think about their commitment to Sherwin. These guys had never before seen visitors in their entire life, let alone Americans who came to bring a message of hope and love to their village. These two friends stuck with Sherwin. They were compassionate and understanding and cared more for him and his well-being than for these people with light skin and unusual hair colors.

Their willingness to remain with their friend, no matter what, changed my life.

We need to be like these two friends. When people are going through a dark time, when their world has turned upside-down, when they've made a costly decision, when their heart is broken, when they feel lost, we need to stay with them. Hold their hand. Or sit with them, not saying a word. Or pray for them. Or listen. Or call to check in on them.

We need one another. God is a relational God. He designed us to be in community. He designed us to live in relationship with Him first and foremost, and then with others. This is what the church is supposed to be. It's not about four walls and a pretty sanctuary. It's about the people we do life with. We need friends who are going to have our backs, who are going to support us and share the truth in love. We need friends who can carry us when we're weak. We need friends we can count on. I love this verse: "And if one can overpower him who is alone, two can resist him. A cord of three strands is not quickly torn apart."[1] This is God's reminder that we are not meant to do life alone.

I remember right after I graduated college, getting ready to turn pro, my friend Kevin, who was still in school, called me after he got out of class. I could tell from his voice he was pretty shaken up, almost like he had been crying.

"What's going on, bro?" I asked, concerned.

Overcome with emotion, he told me he was so angry because one of his classmates started saying a bunch of terrible things about me. "It took everything not to punch this guy in the face," Kevin said, still fuming. As we talked for a bit, I realized that this was a friend who would always have my back. He was loyal and he cared for me, "a friend who sticks closer than a brother."[2]

When I was released from the Patriots, the encouraging and supportive words my loved ones gave meant the world to me. I'll never forget what they said: "We love you. It doesn't matter if you play for another team or if you never play at all. You are still and will always be Timmy to us, and we will always love you."

When I was having a rough time in New York, I treasured the weekends my friends Brad, Kevin, and others would visit. Most times we wouldn't do much except hang out, watch movies, and play video games. The most important thing was just being with them, laughing and goofing off with the guys who loved me for me, not for football. And when I was cut from the Jets, they, and others, were the ones who encouraged me to be patient. "Your time is going to come," they said. "Don't doubt yourself. You have the skill set you need. You can do this. Just keep trusting God."

I am so grateful for the friends in my life. They love me for who I am, not what I do. And they understand me enough to know what's best for me. I'm a pretty intense guy. Very rarely can I sit still for longer than a few minutes; I always have to be doing something. Knowing this, my friends challenge me to slow down, take it easy, and rest.

The Illusion of Independence

"No man is an island" is the famous line written by the poet John Donne.

Contrary to that well-known statement is our human tendency to draw inward, to do life by ourselves, especially when we're going through something painful or hard. We say things like "I don't need anyone" or "I can get through this on my own."

I think most of us have said these words, or something along those lines, at some point in our lives. We do this for many reasons. We were betrayed by someone close to us and don't want to get close to another. We think we should be able to handle pressure, tough times, or trials by ourselves. We don't want to bother anyone. We don't think anyone could help or that they'd even want to.

I mentioned earlier how I was lonely during my time as a New York Jet. While some of the self-isolation was to avoid the media, a part of me was convinced I could white knuckle life on my own. *I'm going to be strong, push through, and fight my pain.* Problem was, the loneliness I struggled with only grew deeper. You know what I didn't realize at the time? That I needed to lean into a loving and supportive community, even if just a few people, and stop believing that I could survive on my own.

Now, I'm not saying we need to shout our every thought, worry, or fear to the world, hoping someone will listen. I'm also not saying we need to air our dirty laundry to a random person to get it off our chest. I'm saying it would do us a world of good to connect with like-minded people who believe in us, who love us, and who are willing to walk with us. Especially during a tough time.

I like what the professional adventurer Bear Grylls said: "A man's pride can be his downfall, and he needs to learn when to turn to others for support and guidance."

Ever since he was a little boy, Brad knew he wanted to be a fireman. He comes from a line of public servants. His father is a police officer, his grandfather a firefighter. After he graduated high school, Brad got a job working with a construction crew to help rebuild a section of New Orleans after the city was destroyed by Hurricane Katrina. It was a great way to help others and make money. After twelve weeks of working twelve to fourteen hours almost each day, Brad was supposed to come home with twelve thousand dollars in his pocket, enough to pay for fire academy and then some.

When the job was over, Brad returned to Florida, expecting his paycheck. He never got the money. The man promised Brad he'd pay him soon, you know, the whole "check's in the mail" bit, but after two months, Brad finally realized he wasn't ever getting paid. He was peeved, ready to find the guy and rip his head off. But he didn't. Brad worked hard, saved up more money, and eventually put himself through fire academy and EMT school. And while he busted his tail to make the same amount of money that had been stolen from him, he was reminded that he couldn't count on anyone.

This attitude stemmed from his childhood. Brad had a rough upbringing filled with violence and abuse. At a young age, he started to believe that he couldn't depend on those closest to him for love, for stability, for anything a kid needed to live well. But what began as a defense or survival mechanism over time turned into deep-rooted self-reliance, pride. Brad lived by the mantra of counting only on himself to get through life and to do whatever he needed to do. He liked to say, "If I'm betting on anyone, I'm betting on myself."

Brad waited three years for a job as a firefighter. No offers came during that time. While he worked a part-time job, the waiting part was tough. And though he was upset, he gritted his teeth. Isolated himself. Kept friends—and he had a good amount of them—at a comfortable distance. Just far enough away emotionally. And three years later, at the same time he had to get recertified just to continue to wait for a firefighter position, a phone call came.

Brad was at the gym, boxing the life out of a punching bag, when his phone buzzed. A random number. He didn't answer, and the phone kept ringing, the same number. Paying no mind to the persistent caller, Brad continued to throw some pretty lethal punches. Finally, after his phone was silent for a minute or two, his dad's number popped up.

"Hey, Dad," Brad sputtered, the punching bag swinging wildly beside him from the last jab.

"Son," his father said, his voice quiet, scared. "We need to go to the hospital now."

"Who's in the hospital?" Brad asked, oblivious, still burning through his workout.

"I'm sorry, Brad. Your doctor kept trying to call you, but you didn't pick up. So they had to tell me. You have cancer, son. Melanoma. Stage 4."

Brad's knees just about buckled. Flashback to three weeks ago when he finally agreed, after his mother's persistent begging, to get a lump on his side checked out. Never in his wildest dreams would he have expected the biopsy to return positive for cancer. Brad wondered how it was possible. *I feel great. Amazing!* What's crazy to me is that he didn't worry about it. He wasn't even that upset. And he definitely didn't feel sorry for himself. Brad just wanted to move forward with the recommended surgery and "get this over and done with." Yeah, that's the survival mechanism talking.

During surgery, doctors discovered the cancer had spread to his lymph nodes. They removed what malignant tissue they could and for the next six months targeted the rest with chemotherapy and radiation. While the treatments, ultimately, were successful and today Brad is cancer free, he had to put a hold on getting recertified as a firefighter. His future looked bleak.

Brad felt all-around battered by life and started to realize that his pride, his hardened attitude of self-reliance wasn't working. Not anymore. And this was when he finally understood that he couldn't do life on his own. He needed God, and he needed others.

Brad says, "My brothers and sisters in Christ helped me through the times I was worn out and could no longer rely on myself to get me through. They not only lifted me up in prayer but also made me realize that I had never been on my own nor did I ever have to be on my own again. To know you have such an amazing support system makes it very easy to put your own ego and pride aside and open your eyes to the blessings that God has been trying to show you all along. I learned who my friends are."

Charles Dickens wrote, "No one is useless in this world who lightens the burdens of another." Friends can encourage us. Motivate us. Inspire us. Celebrate with us. Mourn with us. Listen to us. Make us laugh. Offer a new perspective. Hold us accountable. The benefits of friendship are endless.

If you're going through a tough time, it's important to lean into others for support, for love, for wisdom and encouragement. I've had to do this often in my career lows, and I'm grateful for that support system. In the process, I've also found that every person in my life has unique innate gifts and characteristics. Consequently, each one's role in friendship is different.

One of my friends is business savvy, and we often discuss business matters. I can count on another friend for deep conversations where we wrestle with tough decisions. What ultimately matters is that my friends are loyal, have my best interests in mind, and love me without strings. I strive to be that type of friend to others.

True friendship is about trust, being vulnerable and sharing, not shutting down because of pride. It's about enduring with them. Believing with them. Loving them. And encouraging them.

Today Brad is living a new vision, helping dreams come true at our foundation. God is using what he went through to teach the next generation. He didn't waste Brad's life or take away his dream. He changed Brad's heart and gave him an opportunity to make a difference in a new way.

WHAT WE CAN DO

Let's flip the switch for a minute. How many times have we gotten stuck on ourselves and our problems, that place where we think,

- *The world is so unfair.*
- *Why is life so hard?*
- *Why does it seem I'm the only one going through a rough time?*

Sometimes we can get so caught up in this kind of mental funk that we forget that those around us are going through a hard time. Sometimes we just need, even for a minute, to stop. Step outside of ourselves. Pay attention to the world around us. And do something, no matter how small, to lighten someone's load. It's about perspective.

I think about being cut so many times and not continuing to live my dream of being a quarterback in the NFL. I could easily wallow in that place of self-pity. And sometimes I have. But in the big picture, it almost seems silly. Who cares that I'm not playing football right now? There are millions of children all over the world who dream about something so simple as getting a new pair of flip-flops. Flip-flops! Do you know how many pairs I own?

Perspective.

It's amazing what happens when we help someone when we're feeling helpless. This doesn't have to be some big task or a save-the-world project. You don't have to raise a million dollars. You don't have to go on a mission trip next week. (Although these are all great things, and if you want to, by all means, go for it.)

Think simple. In terms of those around you, send an encouraging text to a friend. Take time to listen, really listen, to another. Make some chicken soup for someone who is sick. Instead of blabbing on and on about your problems, find out what another person is going through. Pray for someone instead of always asking that person to pray for you.

You know what's so awesome about thinking about others instead of focusing on ourselves all the time? It's actually good for us. *Forbes* recently featured an article that talked about how helping others reduces our own stress levels.[3] Emily Ansell of Yale University School of Medicine offered, "Our research shows that when we help others we can also help ourselves. . . . Stressful days usually lead us to have a worse mood and poorer mental health, but our findings suggest that if we do small things for others . . . we won't feel as poorly on stressful days."[4]

Ralph Waldo Emerson said, "The purpose of life is not to be happy. It is to be useful, to be honorable, to be compassionate, to have it make some difference that you have lived and lived well."[5] We do this by reaching out, by finding a need, however small, and filling it (more on this in the last three chapters). It doesn't matter what person we do this for: friends, family, or total strangers. What matters is doing something outside of ourselves.

WHO'S IN YOUR CIRCLE?

You've already read about how I reached out to my circle of trust when I was cut from the Patriots, the Jets, and the Eagles. But I depend on this tight-knit bunch of family and loved ones for more than just hearing encouragement or support. They help me bring clarity when I'm stuck on a decision. And they tell me the truth, even if I don't want to hear it.

Do you have people in your life who will love you enough to speak truth into you? Or hold you accountable? Or challenge you to do the right thing? Or do those around you simply tell you whatever you want to hear or influence you to do things that might be convenient but are questionable from an ethical or moral position?

I think about the opportunity I had to host a TV show. It was a great gig that paid a great chunk of money and only required a few dates of commitment. I talked to my circle-of-trust folks. After each person on the line shared his or her thoughts, the consensus was that it was a good thing. Easy decision, right? The problem was, I later found out that I'd already previously committed to a speaking engagement on one of the days I would be filming for this show.

One of my agents, who was pushing me to say yes, told me, "Just don't show up to the event."

I was floored. "Are you kidding me? These people are counting on me!"

I knew my answer. And barring a medical emergency or something crazy like that, I couldn't just back out. And I definitely wasn't going to not show up.

Though my agent was convinced that the show was too good to pass up, I decided, and my friends and loved ones agreed, I'd have to turn down the opportunity. In hindsight, it was the right decision.

I've made countless phone calls to my circle of trust. And sometimes, in hearing so many different opinions, perspectives, and thoughts, I end the phone call with much more information than I started out with. When I'm armed with different points of view, at times it's even harder to make a decision. But I know I'm wiser for it. And this is what is important. Like Proverbs 13:20 says, "He who walks with wise men will be wise, but the companion of fools will suffer harm."

Who's in your circle of trust? It doesn't have to be a big group of people. It works if you just have two or three people that you can trust, count on to pray for you, wrestle with you on big decisions, and offer wise advice. These are people who are going to tell you the truth, what you need to hear, rather than what you want to hear.

Sometimes you need someone to remind you to dig deep with God, to keep up the faith, to stay in the fight. It's easy to become complacent because life gets in the way. When tough times come or we get stuck in the routine of the dailies, we can forget what matters. And it can be pretty easy to stop growing spiritually, to stop talking to God, and stop learning about the faith walk.

I remember when I first signed on with the Denver Broncos. I had just started my career in the NFL. I was living in a new city. I was with a new team. I was training nonstop. Life was definitely busy. Because of my hectic schedule, I couldn't go to church every week. But I needed spiritual support. My friend Erik would call me every single day, no matter what city I was in or the time-zone difference, and lead me in a devotional and prayer. We did this in good times and in bad, when we were sick, tired, frustrated, or didn't feel like it. I craved the consistency. And I appreciated his willingness to invest in me spiritually.

This is what it means to be surrounded by people you trust and who have your back. Now, keep in mind, I'm not telling you to befriend a group of holy rollers who pride themselves for always wearing a tie and going to Bible study five days a week—and judge you for not doing so. What matters is being surrounded by people who speak truth into you, who support you when you feel weak, and who encourage you when you feel like you just can't do it anymore. (It goes without saying that you should strive to be this kind of friend to others.) Having people like this in your life helps you live at your best. It helps you strive to be better than average, more than ordinary, far above normal.

7

WHO SAID NORMAL IS THE GOAL?

**If you are always trying to be normal,
you will never know how amazing you can be.**

—MAYA ANGELOU

t was supposed to be a routine ultrasound. The kind in which a mother goes gaga over pictures of her baby in utero, posting them proudly on her fridge right when she gets home. But that day, neither mother nor baby came home.

Discovering the thirty-week-old baby wasn't moving, the doctor ordered an emergency cesarean section, a decision that saved the little one's life. Gray in complexion and pleading for breath, Robyn was born on February 21, 2000, weighing only two pounds, ten ounces. She could practically fit inside her parents' hands.

Doctors weren't optimistic. They told Robyn's parents she was probably not going to live. Miraculously, the baby girl defied the odds. Though she survived and was able to leave the NICU after a month, Robyn was diagnosed with cerebral palsy (CP), a neurological disorder that impairs movement and mobility. Though there are varying degrees of CP, one in three afflicted can't walk, one in four has difficulty or can't talk, and three in four experience chronic pain.[1]

When she was three, Robyn learned to walk with the assistance of a walker and knee braces. Tough and determined, she walked everywhere. She even learned how to ride a bike, one with three wheels because she couldn't balance. Though she doesn't remember falling much when she was younger, Robyn remembers how traumatic the aftermath always was. It wasn't that she hurt herself to the point of needing medical attention. She couldn't physically get back up and had to lie on the ground helpless until someone came and picked her up.

Robyn has endured multiple, painful Botox injections to help temporarily relax her muscles, surgeries, weekly physical therapy, and chronic pain every morning. Though this had always been her normal and she never thought of herself as different, when she was in seventh grade, a classmate made fun of the way she walked. "For the first time, I realized that a walker wasn't normal," Robyn says. "I no longer saw it as something that gave me the gift of freedom but a magnet that attracted stares from strangers and sympathetic tones from people I didn't know that well. Some days, all I could focus on was the walker. And when I looked in the mirror, I didn't see a teenage girl, I saw what I was convinced everyone else saw: a disability."

Robyn was fifteen when I met her briefly at our Celebrity Golf Classic, an annual foundation event where we host a weekend of fun and entertainment for our kids and friends of mine.

After a long day of meet-and-greets and swinging clubs, I walked over to the autograph area where I was scheduled to sign books, footballs, and other memorabilia. The place was a madhouse. Many people who crowded the line looked impatient. Some of them even started pushing and shoving, trying to get ahead, not enough to create total chaos but enough for me to notice. I arched my head to the side, trying to glimpse how far back the line ran, when

I caught sight of a blond-haired young lady. She was leaning on a walker. Even through the crowd I could see metal braces that covered her legs. She seemed peaceful, content, oblivious to the people behind and in front of her who were trying to push their way toward the front of the line. It boggled my mind that the point of this particular event was to honor kids with special needs and disabilities, and here these people were invading this girl's space and practically knocking her over so they could fling books and footballs at me to sign.

It reminded me how we often miss what's right in front of us. I speak at a lot of events, to crowds in the hundreds and thousands. I realize that I don't see every single person who attends. But for some reason that day, I noticed this young lady in the masses. Just like I noticed Sherwin and his friends. I stopped signing photographs and made my way toward her. As I got close, her eyes lit up. And frankly, so did mine.

"Hi, I'm Timmy," I said. "I'm so glad you're here!"

"I'm Robyn, with a 'y,'" she replied cheerfully. "I'm so grateful that you would come over and say hi to me." *Grateful?* I thought. I was embarrassed that she had to endure such an unnecessary racket when instead she should have been the one receiving the attention.

For just a few minutes, Robyn shared her story with me. I wished we had more time to talk, but I asked if I could stay in touch. A few months later, we granted her a W15H, one of my favorites. I celebrated her and her family in Atlanta with a special dinner, a spa day, and a VIP tour of the College Football Hall of Fame with an experience catered specifically to her love of the Florida Gators! Robyn and I spent hours talking. She told me that the past few months had been particularly overwhelming. The constant stares at her walker reminded her in a painful way that she wasn't normal. I was heartbroken that over the course of her life Robyn had to listen to people, some directly and others through offhanded comments, tell her she wasn't special. That she didn't fit in.

I tried my best to encourage her. "Robyn, normal is average. Being different is what makes you special and can give you the courage to treat others special," I said, as her eyes brimmed with tears. "God loves you, and you don't have to worry about anything else."

Robyn sent us the sweetest text after that great weekend, words I'll treasure forever. I was taken aback when she called me her "quarterback who made my dreams come true, forever impacting my life in the process." I'm not a quarterback on an NFL team right now, but I'm playing for Robyn. And to me, being on that team, and others like hers, is what matters.

One year later, Robyn surprised me at the next Celebrity Golf Classic, sharing with a crowd of affluent and influential supporters a letter she wrote to me. I love what she said that night. "I used to think that my CP made me different in the worst way, but I have come to realize that my differences don't make me strange; they make me beautiful. Today, instead of seeing my walker as a problem or a hindrance, I see it as a platform to influence lives; it's a way for me to inspire others."

Though Robyn still uses a walker and knee braces to get around, though she still notices the stares that follow her when she is out in public, though she still hears the voices of strangers who draw incorrect conclusions about her, Robyn is not bothered by being different. Though some days are easier than others, she is not defined by what others think, by society's definition of normal, or by those who say she is not special because she has CP. In fact, Robyn appreciates *not* being just like everybody else.

WHAT'S NORMAL, ANYWAY?

Many spend their lives wondering if they're normal or wanting to be, hoping to fit in. To be part of the crowd. You probably experienced this tension in middle and high school. To feel a sense of belonging, you wore the same jeans, the same backpack, and the same hairstyle as everyone else. Or maybe you liked the same music, hated the same classes, and acted as bored or dramatic as those around you. Beyond those tough teenage years, the pull to belong and be normal still impacts the life journey.

It's funny, the particulars of being normal are always changing. Although the word technically means "conforming to the standard or the common type; usual; regular," it means something different depending on the ever-changing whims of society, culture, and generations. One minute playing video games is the "in" thing. The next it's volunteering. One minute the "in" thing is to live in a McMansion; the next day it's buying a tiny house that's under three hundred square feet.

The essence of normal is the status quo, being just like everyone else—in how we look, what we wear, what we like, what we buy, what we watch, where we go on vacation, what we do for fun. Being normal is safe. And easy. It doesn't require much work or effort or change on our part. But it always leads to mediocrity.

When we strive to be just like everyone else, we never have a chance to be special. When you start to embrace and even celebrate how special and different God made you, you can begin to do extraordinary things. You can begin to see yourself through His eyes. You can begin to live in the uniqueness with which you were created. You can be motivated and inspired to go against the grain.

What does that mean? When everyone around you is picking on someone, stand up for that person. When everyone around you is using foul language, say kind things. When you see injustice and everyone else turns a blind eye, try to make it right. Going against the norm can also mean having a different outlook on life than others. When everyone around you is working eighty hours a week so they can one day retire and start enjoying life, you can do something different to start living well in the moment. And instead of keeping up with the Joneses, you can be grateful for what you have right now.

You matter too much to God to be just like everyone else.

CELEBRATE UNIQUE

I'm so thankful I am dyslexic. Yes, you read that right. I'm grateful for this learning disability. Keep in mind, however, I didn't always feel this way. When I was seven years old, I struggled to read. It was hard. My parents determined I was dyslexic, which simply means I process things differently. I'm a tactile learner and have better success grasping concepts and ideas hands-on versus reading about them.

When I was twelve or thirteen years old, I was convinced this learning challenge was the worst thing in the world. *Why can't I just pick up a book and read it like everyone else? Why does it have to take me hours and hours?* Spelling, memorizing, taking timed tests with essays—these things were nightmares. Going into high school, I wondered if I'd pass algebra, be able to take the SATs, and even make it through college. If you told me when I was young that I'd not only graduate college but also maintain a 3.7 GPA, I'd have laughed in your face. I am so grateful for Susan Vanderlinde, my tutor growing up, whose knowledge and compassion made the learning process so much easier. She was a blessing!

Having a learning or any other type of disability doesn't mean you're dumb. Both Albert Einstein, the father of the atomic age, and Thomas Edison, the greatest inventor in history, were dyslexic. Now, I'm not comparing myself to these geniuses by any stretch of the imagination. They happen to be telling examples of what's possible when you understand and utilize the way you were created to process things instead of conforming to everyone else's learning style.

I'm excited to be able to encourage kids and even adults who struggle with dyslexia. I know that God is using that challenge as part of my platform. That's what He does. He takes something we see as a disability, a defect, or a mistake and gives us opportunities to help others who struggle in those same areas. This is what Robyn has learned. She doesn't look at cerebral palsy as an impediment but as a platform through which she can impact the lives of others.

I have never woken up once in my life saying I wanted to be normal, average. I never wanted to be like anyone else. I always wanted to be special. Much of this outlook stemmed from my parents' constant encouragement as long as I can remember. They repeatedly told me and my siblings,

"God has a special plan for you."

"You are not like everyone else."

"You are unique."

Having this ingrained in my head helped to lay a solid foundation of identity in my life. I never saw the point of being normal. Now, I know not all parents are encouraging or supportive. But just because we may not have been told how special we are from our family doesn't mean that we're not; we just might have to work harder to believe it.

It's time to circle back to our identity in God. He created each of us in a unique way for a reason. We are each different in how we look, how we think, how we create, how we process information. We also have different life experiences, good or bad. If you were born with a disability, if you experienced a traumatic upbringing, if you don't have the same social graces as Mr. Popularity down the hall, if you struggle with a learning or a physical disability, it can be tempting to say things like

"God must have made a mistake."

"I want to be someone else."

"I wasn't created the way I should have been."

God would disagree.

I like to think of parts of the Bible as a collection of love letters He wrote for His children. One of them powerfully paints a picture of how wonderful we are, of how special He purposely made us. In this psalm, the writer reflects on this truth. Read it out loud as if you wrote these words.

For You [God] formed my inward parts;
You wove me in my mother's womb.
I will give thanks to You, for I am fearfully and wonderfully made;
Wonderful are Your works,
And my soul knows it very well.
My frame was not hidden from You,
When I was made in secret,
And skillfully wrought in the depths of the earth;
Your eyes have seen my unformed substance;
And in Your book were all written
The days that were ordained for me,
When as yet there was not one of them.

How precious also are Your thoughts to me, O God!
How vast is the sum of them!
If I should count them, they would outnumber the sand.[2]

Whatever obstacles you are facing, whatever struggle you have with not fitting in, whether you feel you aren't pretty enough, strong enough, big enough, fast enough, or smart enough, know that God created you perfect. You are wonderfully made. You are skillfully made. You are not an accident. You are not a mistake.

Don't get beat down by the stares, whispers, or obnoxious opinions of others who point out how different you are, look, or act. They don't know God's plan for your life. They don't know how God can use what they may view as a weakness. If you focus on how much you hate those scars or those burns, you might miss the opportunity to encourage or inspire someone else who is going through a similar journey. If you feel like a weirdo because you're super shy, you might miss out on appreciating the gift of reflection God gave you. When you begin to accept how God purposely created you, you can begin to appreciate your uniqueness and allow Him to use those gifts.

God gave you whatever challenges you have for a reason. If you're feeling discouraged, trust His character. Trust that He has your best interest at heart. He has a better outcome for your life than you can imagine. His love is perfect. And He loves you perfectly. We may see ourselves as unworthy, unusable, flawed, or broken, but God looks at us as shining stars. He thinks about us all the time, countless thoughts that are precious, beloved.

Often, we make the mistake of comparing God to someone who represents Him, either poorly or wonderfully. Problem is, because we're human, we may mirror God's heart beautifully one day and pretty awfully the next. I'm the same person, but I can leave a good example for one person and a bad example for another, depending on their perspective and my attitude and actions at the time I'm around them. You can encounter one pastor, teacher, or leader who is kind, encouraging, and gracious and another who is judgmental, impatient, or selfish. Don't let your relationship with God and your ideas about Him stem from those who represent Him.

It may not be the easiest thing to do each day, but trust God and His heart for you. Know that He's got a plan. Know that there is something beautiful and purposeful about what you may perceive as a shortcoming.

What You Have to Offer

When I talk about how special each one of us is, I'm not talking about the way society sees us. We are not special just because we graduated from an Ivy League school and others find that impressive. Or that we're excellent performers, own a successful business, or excel at pretty much whatever we put our minds to do.

I'm talking about the uniqueness with which we were created, the gifts, talents, and abilities that make up who we are. Many of us get bogged down in life because we compare ourselves to others and fall short. I've mentioned this throughout this book because it's a common human struggle. Instead of worrying about not being as great of a public speaker, as great of a writer, as smart, as compassionate, or as creative as someone else, we have to maximize what we have to offer.

Think about what you're good at, the unique traits that are hardwired in you. Think about what you love to do. Maybe you are a talented musician or athlete. You may have a unique way of teaching others or great communication skills. You may be compassionate, charismatic, or an amazing host. You might be a strategic thinker, skilled at building things, or creative.

Instead of wanting to be like someone else, make the most of your talents. The Bible teaches us that "as each one has received a special gift, employ it in serving one another as good stewards of the manifold grace of God."[3]

Use what He has given you. Hone your skills. Work on them. Don't let them waste away. Whether it's singing, speaking, serving, teaching, working with numbers, or cooking, use it to make an impact on this world. Oftentimes, when we get stuck playing the comparison game, we let our God-given gifts and abilities lie dormant.

My friend Judah says, "The Christian faith is about living life with an open hand, using the gifts and blessings in our lives for others. Like a conveyor belt, we simply get to touch the blessings and the gifts as they keep moving out toward others. We are blessed to be a blessing. When we stop the flow, the blessings stop." Don't hold on to your gifts. Share them. Use them to serve. Use them to aim above the status quo and make a difference.

Don't strive to be like someone else. Be who God created you to be. Be you.

One more thing. Let God be God. Allow Him to use what you bring to Him however He chooses. There's nothing wrong with dreaming big. I do this all the time! But how God ultimately orchestrates the plan of your life through these gifts is up to Him. You might love basketball and play the game well, but you might not be the next LeBron James.

Work on your gifts and talents in a way that challenges you. Don't compare your skill level to anyone else. When we do this, sometimes it makes us want to give up. I hear this all the time: "If I can't be the best at something, why bother?" Why bother practicing the piano if I'm never going to make it into Julliard? Why bother writing if my book will never hit the *New York Times* Best Sellers list? It's okay to want to be the best, but it's more important to want to be *your* best.

I promise you this: God will use your giftings and abilities in His way and for His plan. It might be to influence one person or one million. Rather than focus on trying to figure out or influence how He will make it happen, focus on Him.

The Problem of Pride

While some people may struggle with not knowing what they have to offer, others know exactly what that is and forget that "every good thing given and every perfect gift is from above, coming down from the Father" (James 1:17).

I'll always remember one particular Sunday at church with my family. I was in the third grade, a kid with a beastly competitive streak. While God had blessed me with athletic skill, as a child I wasn't mature enough to realize this was a talent He had given me. Oh sure, I was schooled in the Bible and the principles of Jesus and knew the truth in my head; the problem had to do with my heart. At the time, my passion for scoring touchdowns, hitting home runs, and winning games superseded the knowledge in my head.

After the church service, my parents stopped to talk to some friends, a couple who had four kids, similar in ages to my siblings. Unfortunately, this family didn't have a child my age, so I stood idly by, watching Peter trying to flirt with one of the girls and my sisters chatting it up with two other siblings, one of whom had a crush on my sister Katie. Hoping to get in with the older kids, I tried to pry my way into their conversation. For the life of me I can't remember exactly what I said, but I know with certainty that it was stupid, arrogant. I blurted out, without any context whatsoever, something along the lines of "I'm better in baseball than everyone in my grade" and, directing my attention to the two guys my sisters were talking to, "I'm sure I can beat you too!" To add insult to injury, I announced this in my loudest, most confident voice.

I told you, not too smart.

As soon as that last word flew out of my mouth, my two sisters looked at me, horrified. My heart sank. I knew in that moment I had disappointed them deeply. These were two people that I looked up to so much. Katie was always so much fun and awesome to hang with, and Christy, always full of wisdom and a great role model. These were two of the coolest people on the planet. I was so embarrassed. I flashbacked to being four or five, when after winning a handful of T-ball games and blabbing to anyone and everyone within earshot about my wins, Mom and Dad instituted a new house rule. Before each game, I had to memorize a Bible verse about humility. Every. Single. Game.

I don't know what possessed me to make that proud statement that Sunday, but it seems in that moment I forgot about everything my parents had taught me about being humble, like pride coming before a fall, doing "nothing from selfishness or empty conceit," and how pride brings a person low (see Proverbs 16:18, Philippians 2:3, and Proverbs 29:23).

My sisters were so appalled by my behavior, they didn't say a word to me for the longest time. I can picture vividly the walk from the church to our car, which was probably a good quarter of a mile. I lagged behind, feeling ashamed. And small. All I had wanted to do was to look cool in front of my two big sisters, fit in with the older kids. And I thought I could impress them by saying something impressive about myself. As I trudged toward the car, afraid that my foolish actions would make them never want to talk to me again, I said to myself with conviction, *I am never ever going to say something stupid like that again.*

Look, there's a way to show confidence and self-belief without being prideful. Growing up I traveled with my dad to hundreds of baseball games and tournaments. If he wasn't overseas sharing the love of Jesus, he was driving me to play ball all over the state of Florida and around the country. Before and after games, we'd have countless honest conversations. I could share with my dad things I couldn't necessarily say to my teammates or coaches. These talks required depth, and they are some of my favorite memories with Dad. I may have had to put on a game face in front of my team, but once I sank into the passenger seat of his car and slammed the door shut, I could tell him how my coach made what I thought was a dumb call or how the pitcher on the opposing team was incredible.

After each game, Dad would always ask how I thought I did. I was honest. Sometimes I admitted I thought I was the best; other times I told him I was discouraged because I didn't play my best. Dad was and is my biggest champion and believer. He was always honest and never doled out fake compliments. He struck the perfect balance of encouraging me and telling me I was the best and also reminding me to keep working harder.

When we gloat, boast, or show off the talents, gifts, and abilities that God has given us, it shreds our true identity. We forget whose we are. We forget from whom our blessings come. We take credit for what God ultimately did in us. The Bible challenges, "For who regards you as superior? What do you have that you did not receive? And if you did receive it, why do you boast as if you had not received it?"[4]

In sports or the entertainment industry, it's easy to want to point to ourselves and show the world how awesome we performed. After all, wins and awards require work. And when you put in the work, there is a tendency to want to show off.

While self-confidence is important and we should believe we can achieve great things, there must be a balance. We must be proud of our accomplishments without letting them define us. Accolades don't last. You may have been named Most Likely to Succeed in high school, but the next year, nobody cares. There is always going to be another winner after you. This is why we need to live knowing whose we are. When we fix our identity in the One who created us, we can keep pride at bay. And we can redirect whatever praise may come our way to the One worthy of it.

BEING MORE THAN AVERAGE REQUIRES COURAGE

True story: A man I'll call John was walking to the local PDQ to grab a bite to eat. Just as he stepped into the parking lot, a young man with special needs, a visible scar on his neck, and facial deformities approached him. As he had recently injured his foot, John was wearing a walking boot. The young man initiated the conversation by asking, "What happened to your foot?"

"I hurt it working out," John replied, a bit suspicious about why a stranger would strike up a conversation in a parking lot.

"Can I pray for you?" the young man asked.

The question startled John. In fact, his first and immediate thought was, *What a weirdo!* But a split second later, he was quick to realize how courageous the young man was to ask a stranger if he could pray for him. And John felt humbled, admiring the guy for daring to do something different.

"Sure," John responded. "I would appreciate it." Though he assumed the young man would walk away and pray for him in the privacy of his own home, that's not what happened. In John's own words, "What made this guy even more courageous was that he got down on his knee, placed a hand on my boot, and prayed right there. It made me realize that when you're doing things for the greater good, there is no need to be embarrassed or ashamed or wonder how people are going to perceive you, because the only opinion that matters comes from above."

I love the bold spirit of this young man, who, not knowing how his act of compassion would be received, determined to do something extraordinary. And what began as a simple question impacted John in a positive way.

When is the last time you did something different? Something beyond your comfort zone? Something that wasn't familiar but could do a world of good in the life of another? When you stay put in your comfort zone, you don't grow. You don't stretch. You're not challenged. You stay the same. Stagnant.

My parents did a phenomenal job of constantly pushing me outside my comfort zone. When I first balked at speaking in public, my parents took notice. And they signed me up for every activity that required me to stand in front of a crowd and talk, even sing. They made me pray out loud in front of others. They made me give presentations at science fairs. They signed me up for church plays, which were big productions performed in front of thousands of people. They even made me sing in the choir. I did what I was told, even if I didn't want to. Public speaking at an early age was not fun. Mom and Dad weren't being mean, though, or setting me up to fail. They were helping me overcome my fears. When you are constantly challenged outside your comfort zone, eventually you become comfortable in that larger space.

When I was in the eighth grade, as part of a missions outreach, my youth group visited an arcade crammed with thirty or so young people playing Skee-Ball, pinball, and air hockey. One of the leaders asked us kids, "Who wants to get up and preach?"

All eyes fell to the floor and stayed there. I volunteered. I didn't necessarily want to or feel inspired, but no one else raised a hand. At the same time I said yes, a slew of thoughts ran through my head. *What if I forget what I'm supposed to say? What if my words come out wrong? What if no one listens? What if they laugh at me?* When it was time to talk, even as fear weighed heavily on me, I spoke from the heart. My words may not have been eloquent and I may not have communicated the message with perfection, but I was sincere. And if I remember correctly, a handful of people responded positively to the message of Jesus.

Even today I sometimes get nervous speaking in public. It's because I care about the outcome. I want to do my best for God and for everyone who is listening. When we do something that stretches who we are, that demands courage, that pulls us into unfamiliar territory, we grow. And most times it'll be worth it. Note, I'm not talking about bungee jumping off the Empire State Building or quitting the job you need to feed your family so you can try out for some reality television show. I'm talking about doing something uncommon that can make a difference.

It's okay to feel afraid while taking the first step. I love the title of the book *Feel the Fear . . . and Do It Anyway!* Doing something against the flow of culture, society, or the crowd will probably feel uncomfortable and scary. Do it anyway.

I think about the men Jesus took under His wing, the unorthodox group of fishermen, tax collectors, and revolutionaries. I wonder if they hesitated when Jesus asked if they would follow Him. Maybe Peter thought for a brief moment he might be better off with his fishing business than following someone who, though intriguing, was making some pretty controversial statements. Maybe the tax man thought it'd be easier to stay put in his cushy office, guiding others how to make the most of their deductions. I can't help but think some of the disciples may have wrestled with the decision to follow Jesus, feeling pulled to keep doing what they were doing, to move in cadence with the flow of the crowd.

And I wonder what the Pharisees thought of Jesus. Maybe one of them, while walking around town in his fancy robes, puffing out his chest, paused, just for a minute, and thought, *Hmm, there's something different about this man. I've seen Him perform miracles. I've seen Him heal people. Maybe I should talk to Him, see what He's about instead of beating Him senseless over the head with this rules-and-regulations business.* But then, as another religious hotshot sidled up to him and started talking shop, condemning some guy down the street for breaking the Sabbath, he brushed away those thoughts. And in choosing to ignore the gnawing of his conscience for the sake of belonging to the tight-knit brotherhood of the Pharisees, he continued to keep in step with those around him.

Euripides, one of the greatest authors of the Greek tragedies, wrote, "There is just one life for each of us: our own."

Be who God created you to be. And stand out for the right reason. Don't fight against what's right or what's possible just to get approval or applause from others. And don't hide or stay quiet for the sake of not making waves and being just like everyone else.

Be bold. Brave. Courageous.

8

STAND UP

**If you don't stand for something,
you'll fall for anything.**

—Unknown

About a thousand high-school kids flocked to the campgrounds. I'd never seen so many teenagers in one place in my life. It was my first time being at a Christian camp that hosted multiple churches. It was also my first time being around high schoolers. A few weeks shy of fifteen, I wasn't intimidated by the crowd. I felt confident. I was going to dominate. I was going to get to know people. I was going to talk to a bunch of girls. And I was going to crush every one of the week's many sports competitions.

I was excited to be at that camp for a few reasons—not just for the five hundred or so girls that I could potentially meet. My brothers were there too. Peter, who was a senior in high school at the time, was one of the older kids, and Robby, one of three hundred counselors. It was like the dream team. My brothers and I were prepared to destroy the camp, metaphorically speaking. And in a good way. For us alpha males, at least.

My brothers, both great athletes, and I were particularly stoked for the basketball tournament. It was the event that attracted the most attention. While I was bummed to not be on Robby's team, Peter and I were on the same team, which had some pretty decent athletes. We weren't great, but we were tough. We shared the mind-set that although we may not win, whoever we played was guaranteed to go through hell to beat us. Peter is a beast. He's scrappy and will do whatever it takes to win. Trust me, I know this from wrestling with him my whole life. Let's just say it took more than being five feet eleven and 170 pounds soaking wet to make 172 tackles in his senior year of high school playing football for the state championship–winning team.

I think it was Mark Twain who said, "It's not the size of the dog in the fight. It's the size of the fight in the dog." Well, Peter's got a lot of fight in him.

The basketball tourney started out with forty or so teams, and as the days passed, the bracket got smaller and smaller. Peter and I played our hearts out. No guts, no glory. Our team crushed, clinching our spot in the final four. Robby's team also made it to the semifinals. If they won their game and we won ours, we would play each other in the championship round.

If that happened, it would be the second time I'd face Robby that week. Probably the second-most popular camp event was the arm-wrestling competition. For an hour or two each day, the sounds of grunts through gritted teeth and arms slamming down on tables echoed throughout the gymnasium. Despite being one of the youngest competitors, I took down every guy that sat across from me (you can see why I had to work on that arrogance problem I talked about in the last chapter).

The bracket narrowed to two final players—me and Robby. We sat, poker-faced, staring each other down. Surrounded by hundreds of camp-goers who stood shoulder to shoulder, we were unfazed. I felt a little torn, excited to be able to compete against my big brother but at the same time nervous because I was about to compete against my big brother!

The crowd started chanting "Tebow! Tebow! Tebow!" When the referee shouted, "Go!" I gritted my teeth, pushed as hard as I could, my muscles quivering. Robby looked at me, and for a split second I could see a wash of guilt in his eyes. While he and I fight like typical brothers, he is also super-protective of me. I had a feeling he was thinking, *Dang, I'm beating my baby brother. Maybe I should pull back.* But that split second was over pretty quick. Though he may have been temporarily sympathetic for my plight, his will to win was stronger. More teeth gritting. More grunting. Both of our forearms shaking, Robby's arm pressed firmly over mine, just an inch or two above the table. With his mouth fixed in a deadly grimace and with a powerful grumble, he slammed my arm down. As I groaned in frustration of defeat, Robby reached out and clapped my shoulder. "Are you all right?" he asked, genuinely concerned. "How's your arm?" I wasn't happy about losing, but there was no one else I'd rather lose to.

Back to basketball. The entire camp gathered outside under the lights, wrapped in a blanket of Florida humidity, to watch Robby's team play in the semifinals. The bleachers on both sides of the court were full. Others stood. Everyone watched, eyes glued to the action. Excluding himself, every player on Robby's team was a camper, a high-school student. The opposing team consisted of camp counselors, college kids.

It was a dirty game from the start. I stood near the sidelines watching the drama unfold. It only took a few minutes into the first quarter to notice that the spirit of vicious competition dominated good sportsmanship.

As I watched the opposing team take cheap shots at and body-check my brother and his teammates, my blood boiled. I was furious. Seeing red. I stormed over and stood just under the basket, yelling out in protest. By now, the crowds on either side of me were on their feet cheering or jeering, depending on which team they were rooting for.

The score volleyed back and forth for a while, not more than four points different. For sure, Robby dominated the game, but the opposing team pushed and fouled him continuously along the way. Though my brother was by far the best player in that game, the other guys had the better team. And though he was a force to be reckoned with, matching bucket for bucket, Robby and his teammates ultimately lost.

Then, it was our turn to play. Peter and I took charge of the court, leading our teammates to victory and into the finals. We had barely fifteen minutes before it was time to face the punk team who had beaten Robby's. I didn't care. It might have been my arrogance talking, but I could have run for days. So could Peter. Together, we were unstoppable.

After the tipoff, I ran up and down that court, slamming basket after basket. I may have been just a freshman in high school, but I blasted those college guys. Sure, I wanted to win, but this game was more than that. It was personal. They had played dirty and beaten my brother. I wanted blood—in the form of racking up points.

As I shot a couple of different lay-ups, one of the opposing players shoved me from behind. It was an obvious foul, but no one called it. The refs were counselors and, it seemed, oblivious. I guessed we were playing them too. While I didn't get physical in response, I warned this camp counselor to chill out. He didn't listen.

Both teams engaged in an epic back-and-forth battle, with the other team getting more and more physical with Peter and me in particular. I tried to dodge an elbow here, a shoulder there while scoring point after point. As the opposing players busted out with loud-mouth trash talk, Robby stood on the sidelines, veins popping out of his neck, calling them out for their cheap shots. I scanned the court for a ref, waiting to hear a whistle. Nothing. They still weren't watching.

Bam! I stumbled from the force of someone trying to slam me off my feet. I turned to the player and repeated the warning to chill out. He gave me what he thought was a threatening stone-cold look. With sweat flying off my face, I said to this college dude, "Just trust me. You don't want to do that." I meant it. Football season was only a few weeks away, and I didn't want to get hurt. Peter was also getting ready to play his senior year; he didn't want to get hurt either.

Fourth quarter. Peter stole the ball and took off down the court at full speed. As he ran, an opposing player tackled him from behind. My brother fell to the ground, cutting up his knees and elbows on the rough asphalt. While the crowd went bananas, the guy who pushed Peter stood over him, talking smack. I didn't know what he was going to do next, so I unleashed pure fury. If this dude was turning this into football, I was ready to play that game. I ran toward the guy and put a shoulder in him so forceful it could have shattered an average person's ribs. I meant to hit him, just not that hard.

Then, utter chaos. Seeing Peter on the ground, blood gushing from his knees and elbows, Robby flew onto the court and started taking names. I started tossing anyone who came close to me. I didn't know whether they were coming to calm me down or punch me out, so I naturally took a defensive position. Players on both sides were shoving and pushing. A few counselors stepped onto the court, yelling at full volume and trying to pry us apart. Here's the thing. My brothers and I had no intention of starting a fight. All we wanted to do was protect one another. I wasn't being a bully; I was making a statement: don't ever touch my brother like that again.

Finally, and I can't remember how, tempers cooled down enough so we could finish the quarter. But not before I got kicked out of the game. Guess I wasn't good enough for the counselors who were reffing. And while just before the brawl our team was up 68–62, with Peter hurting and me kicked out of the game, we lost.

That night some of the camp leaders called what I'm almost certain was an impromptu meeting to discuss the chaos that had ensued earlier on the basketball court. Some of the counselors started semi-apologizing, saying that things got a little out of hand, yada-yada. I tuned them out. I had no respect for these guys. They were supposed to be our leaders, in college for Pete's sake. And yet they were the first guys on the court to take competition to a dirty and violent level. These guys were tools.

Okay, fine. So I didn't do a great job that day of showing Jesus. While my character may have been questionable in throwing that guy down on that court, in that moment, catching a glimpse of Peter cut up and lying on the ground with some dude towering over him, I was focused on one thing—standing up for my brother.

In hindsight, yeah, I probably shouldn't have checked that one player and instead just helped Peter up. While I might not have done what mattered most, I showed my brother that he mattered. I chose to take a stand for him. I chose to defend and fight for him. I chose to have his back.

You only get so many moments in life to show people they matter. A coach might get one chance to fight for a player. A teacher might get one chance to fight for the future of a student. You might get one chance to encourage your neighbor before he moves away. You might get one chance to share your faith with a coworker before she gets another job. I'm not saying the way I showed Peter he mattered was necessarily the right way, but my heart was in the right place.

I'm not fifteen anymore, and over the years I've worked on tempering that young arrogance. And though I have a fiercely competitive nature—that'll never change—I strive to keep growing in maturity and stand for things that really matter in the big picture. Like Sherwin and kids like him who have disabilities or illnesses. And obviously, my faith.

I'm a big believer in the statement "If you don't stand for something, you'll fall for anything." What does it mean to take a stand? It's pretty simple. It's standing up for something or someone you believe in. Every single one of us has the power to do that. For the sake of this book, I'm not talking about fighting against a political or social issue, galvanizing a hundred of your closest friends and picketing some organization, company, or product. You don't have to be a social activist that garners national attention.

Standing up is a way of life. Pay attention to opportunities where you can make a positive difference. Impact change. Be a hero every day. Find a need and fill it. You can do this in big ways and small ways.

Another way to figure out what it means for you to take a stand is to ask yourself, *What am I known for?* Are you known for playing video games all day? Punching a clock and binging on Netflix afterward? Are you known for your impatience? Or are you known for standing up for what's right? Loving people? Being generous with your time? Being a faithful friend? Being kind to strangers?

In the last chapter, we talked about how we don't need to be normal just like everyone else. Taking a stand for something is a perfect way to resist staying complacent and being average.

KEEP IT SIMPLE

The stand you take may not be the biggest deal to the entire world, but it can be a big deal for one person. For instance, you don't have to feed all of Africa, but feeding one person can have more of a far-reaching impact than you may realize. So can taking a stand for someone who is getting bullied.

Recently, someone shared with me something he did in middle school that, while he thought wasn't consequential, left a lasting impression. One of his classmates was a loner, autistic. Every single day, a group of bullies would pick on him, push him around, and kick over the wheeled backpack he pulled along. One day this young man, who had watched this for quite some time, reached a breaking point. He approached the leader of the pack and, in a calm and nonconfrontational way, asked him a question: "Why are you doing this?"

Without even knowing it, this young man put the bully on the spot. While the guy didn't say anything in response, neither he nor anyone else ever bothered that autistic kid again. Later, the classmate who was picked on thanked the young man. "For what?" he replied. "I didn't even do anything." Not anything dramatic, that is. He didn't pick a fight. He didn't yell. He didn't have to do anything aggressive. This young man just asked a question. What he chose to do was simple and yet made a significant difference in the life of another.

I've been pretty vocal about my beliefs and have taken stands on many things—even a knee now and then. I've been told many times, "But, Timmy, I just don't know what to take a stand for."

My response? "Have you ever seen someone hurting? Have you ever seen something wrong? Have you ever been confronted by a problem you could fix?"

"Yes, of course" is the reply.

"Well, then help that person. Right that wrong. Be part of the solution." This is what it means to take a stand.

I'll never forget one of the first times I drove into New York City after signing on with the Jets. I was stopped at a red light. Although I was six or seven cars from the intersection, I noticed an older gentleman wearing dark glasses and carrying a white support cane, the kind used by the blind. Surrounding him was classic New York traffic—a sea of beeping taxis, the masses rushing across congested city streets.

Moving maybe a car length or two with each changing light, I watched this man attempt to cross the street three times. Three times he tried to make his way a few steps into the flow of the foot traffic, tapping his cane along the way, but then likely feeling overwhelmed, he'd stop in midstride and take a few steps back toward the curb. Not one person helped this guy cross the street. Not one.

I wanted to get out of the car and help him but was strongly advised not to, because of that whole media-attention thing. Looking back, even though I was several lanes over from where this man was, I should have listened to my gut and made the effort instead of listening to those who told me not to. I regret not doing the right thing.

Sitting in the car that day, watching the scene unfold, I was mad. I remember thinking, *What's the matter with people?* This was a great opportunity for people to get off their phones, stop being distracted, stop checking their Likes on social media, get out of their heads, and take a stand. Yes, even by helping someone who is having trouble getting to his destination. Something that takes only a few minutes to do. Something that doesn't require a college degree, a talent, a skill, or detailed instructions.

Taking a stand doesn't always require a ton of work, effort, or strategy. You don't have to start a foundation or end world hunger. Nor does it need to be this powerful moment where everyone in the room or in the world is watching. It only requires willingness.

Find a need and fill it. Ask God to put something or someone on your heart. Do something different. He will use whatever you are able to offer for the greater good.

WHAT GOD CAN DO

I was in college, getting ready to face Miami, when for the first time I wanted to do something different with my eye black. I was in the training room getting ready to pick up my eye-black strips, when I wondered if I could do something with them that would inspire someone else. I had seen a few players, like Reggie Bush, who had written their area code on their eye blacks.

The first verse that came to mind was Philippians 4:13: "I can do all things through Him who strengthens me." It's a great verse for football and a great verse for life and faith. While this has long been one of my favorites, it's important to note the context in order to fully grasp the meaning of the verse.

In the text leading up to verse 13, Paul, the man who wrote the book of Philippians, says, "I have learned to be content in any circumstance. I have experienced times of need and times of abundance. In any and every circumstance I have learned the secret of contentment" (Philippians 4:11–12, NET). These verses explain that Paul was referring to being content when he followed with "I am able to do all things." He's saying, "I can handle the good. I can handle the bad. I can handle whatever the world can throw at me because my relationship with Jesus is rock solid. He'll see me through the storms." He knew not just how to survive but how to thrive in riches and poverty, good times and bad.

That game, a few people noticed it. I kept putting it on my eye black every week for the rest of the regular season. I remember running out of the tunnel right before we Gators faced Alabama in the 2008 SEC Championship. In my heart I felt God calling me to change the verse, but I wasn't sure to which one. After a few days, the one that kept coming to mind was John 3:16, the essence of God's heart for us: "For God so loved the world, that He gave His only begotten Son, that whoever believes in Him shall not perish, but have eternal life."

When I told my parents about it, Mom was thrilled. Dad, however, was a bit cautious. "You know how Coach likes his routine, Timmy. Don't mess with that," he warned. He was right in that Coach Meyer was a pretty superstitious guy. If we won with our socks pulled up, he'd make a mental note and we'd have to keep them up for the next game. While he hesitated when I first broached the topic, Coach Meyer ultimately gave me his blessing.

On January 8, 2009, during the National Championship game, I wore

"John 3:16" on my eye black. After we defeated Oklahoma, Coach, my parents, and I ate dinner together at a restaurant in Gainesville. As we chowed down, his phone rang. Coach Meyer's responses to whoever was on the other end were curt.

"Yep." Pause.

"Uh-huh." Pause.

"Oh." Pause.

"Okay, then." Pause.

"Good-bye, now."

"Well," he said as he turned to us, nodding, his face stretched in a bit of a smile. "I was just told that ninety-four million people Googled 'John 3:16' during the game!"

Talk about humbling. God is so big that He used something so small, a tiny biblical reference painted under my eyes, to impact people to search His Word.

I wore different verses my senior year. I felt honored when fans started a group on Facebook that rallied the Gator Nation to wear eye blacks during my last home game in the Swamp—many of them with their favorite Bible verse on it. I decided to play in the Senior Bowl, which was my last opportunity to wear a verse under my eyes. In fact, I learned that the NCAA made a new rule banning players from personalizing their eye blacks the next season. Most of the verses I chose made it to the top spot on Google Trends, which told me that many people wanted to know what these verses said.

Exactly three years after wearing "John 3:16" for the first time, I was playing for the Broncos. NFL rules forbade me from wearing personalized messages on my eye blacks, but still, without any help from me, the John 3:16 theme continued. In one of the most memorable games in my career, we beat the heavily favored Steelers 29–23.

Our team's PR guy flagged me down just before my postgame press conference. "Hey, Timmy," Patrick blurted out, his face flushed. "Do you have any idea what happened?"

"Uh, we just beat the Steelers?" I started to say something sarcastic, in a joking manner, but dialed it back when I noticed how serious he looked, like he was about to say something really important.

"Do you know that it was exactly three years since you wore 'John 3:16'? And during this game, you threw for 316 yards. Your yards per completion were 31.6. The time of possession was 31:06. The ratings for the night were 31.6 million. And during the game ninety million people Googled 'John 3:16'!"

Wow. To think that all those years ago, all I had wanted was just to do something different with eye black. I felt so small in that moment. I didn't know it was exactly three years later. And I didn't know what God was doing or that He was even doing anything at all. I was focused on doing what I needed to do to win a playoff game. And as far as the eye black went, it had become habitual, something I did without much thought, like brushing my teeth. It's not like I asked God to do something huge with it.

I was reminded that God is a big God. And He is always at work—with or without me. Just goes to show you that we never know what God can do with the small choices we make, with the stands we take, or with something positive we do even unintentionally.

Please don't think writing something under my eyes was a monumental stand that required a massive amount of courage. Give me a break. We live in a country where 83 percent of the population identifies themselves as Christian.[1] This wasn't an act of bravery. It was an act of doing something different. People in other countries are persecuted for their faith, even killed. Now that's courage in action.

It's amazing what God can do when you are willing to do something different. Some people may not understand what you're doing. Some may question what you're doing. Some may think you're crazy for doing it. But know that God can take that willingness and do amazing things through it, even when you don't have a clue. Because that's how big He is.

STAY TRUE TO WHO YOU ARE

In chapter 3 I talked about my first game starting for the Denver Broncos. Though the Miami Dolphins had crushed us for most of the game, in the fourth quarter, on the verge of getting shut out for the first time since 1992, we turned it around. I helped lead our team to a double-digit comeback to win in overtime. And we won for the first time in the eight games the Broncos played on the Dolphins' field.

This was the kind of comeback moment I dreamed about as a little boy. Improbable victory has always fired me up. So when winning seemed laughable, absolutely out of the question, and our team rallied and flipped our losing streak on its back, I was beside myself.

I'll never forget what happened immediately after Matt Prater nailed the game-winning fifty-two-yard field goal. The field blew up. Every Bronco teammate, coach, and staff member rushed onto the grass while the fans in the stadium went wild. As I ran a few steps onto the field, adrenaline pounding, I got down on one knee, my elbow resting on the other, fist to my forehead, head bowed. Yep, I "Tebowed."

This wasn't a celebration stance. It was a reminder of who was in charge. I had to humble myself in the midst of this victory, remembering and thanking God for everything He'd done for me. The win wasn't about me. Taking a knee and saying a prayer of thanks was a way of keeping my heart in the right place, keeping pride at bay. It was about submitting to God. It wasn't necessarily a public stance for my faith, but something I'd always done with intention.

If you look at some of my pre-NFL games, I took a knee often. I did it after the Gators lost to Alabama in the 2009 SEC Championship. I did it before games in high school. And most times I did it on the sidelines, not drawing attention to myself. Whether in victory or loss, "Tebowing" in my mind turned the attention off of me and pointed toward God.

There is a temptation especially in big moments like miraculous comebacks to get washed away in the attention that follows. I've always wanted to remind myself on purpose that no matter the monumental win or the crushing loss, God is bigger than those things. And bigger than me.

I can't tell you how many people have come up to me and said, "Hey, you're that guy who takes a knee after touchdowns." I just smile and nod my head. Contrary to popular opinion, I've never done that as a touchdown celebration. But the day we beat Miami in overtime and I took a knee as our team and fans celebrated, a cameraman in the midst of the media barrage homed in on me. And for some reason, it spurred a trend.

A Denver native named Jared Kleinstein and a group of his friends were watching the game at a bar in New York City. Noticing my knee stance, he and his crew took a picture of themselves doing the same. After he uploaded the photo to his Facebook account, it started to attract a stream of Likes. In the next few days, Jared created the *Tebowing* Tumblr blog and purchased the Tebowing domain name for ten dollars. Suddenly, Tebowing became the new "planking" phenomenon. Everyone was doing it—celebrities at award shows, high-school students during athletic events, players during NBA games, even presidential candidates. Also, it became an official word in the English language, defined as "the act of 'taking a knee' in prayerful reflection in the midst of an athletic activity."[2] Another definition I've read is "to get down on a knee and start praying, even if everyone else around you is doing something completely different."[3]

While all the hoopla was somewhat flattering (the greatest form of flattery, after all, is imitation), I'm not the first athlete to take a knee and pray or thank God. And it's not like I set out that day purposely to do something that would attract attention. It's funny, the next week when we faced the Detroit Lions, linebacker Stephen Tulloch Tebowed on top of me after he sacked me in the second quarter.

Taking a stand doesn't always mean doing something radical. Sometimes God will use something you've always done in a way that's bigger than you can imagine. Sometimes He'll use something He puts on your heart, or maybe He'll use your convictions, your search for truth, your desire to do the right thing for a greater purpose.

Want to be a stand-taker? Do the right thing. If you're not sure what to do or whom to help, just do what's right. Uphold your standards. Stay true to your faith. Be kind. Be compassionate. Be generous. Stand up for what you believe in.

Standing up for something you believe in is not always easy. You may get some flak. You may get criticized. You may do this alone. Winston Churchill said, "You have enemies? Good. That means you've stood up for something, sometime in your life."[4] While *enemies* might be a strong word, don't get sidetracked by those who don't believe in you or by those who don't understand what it is you are doing. Whenever you dare to do something different, critics of some sort are bound to show up.

And sometimes in the process of standing up for something, you may fail in some way, which will likely attract more critics. Don't let this keep you on the sidelines, away from continuing to participate in God's greater plan.

Taking a Stand Doesn't Mean We Won't Fall

I think of the many people who have stood for something, particularly public figures with a platform, and somewhere along the way made a mistake. Or a bad decision. Or had a lapse in judgment. It saddens me when I hear others criticize them, rip them apart, call them hypocrites or something far worse.

While it's disappointing to hear about a role model falling short, it's disappointing that we actually put others on a pedestal. Here's some truth. Those we look up to are human. They make mistakes. They say the wrong things. And they mess up, sometimes royally. They may try not to, but any time you idolize people and hold up unrealistic expectations you think they should follow, at some point they're going to let you down.

News flash: I'm nowhere near perfect. I try to be a good role model. I try to do and think the right things. But I'm human. I mess up. I have failed and let people down. I certainly don't belong on a pedestal. Frankly, I make a terrible idol. Jesus is the only One who belongs on a pedestal. Jesus is the only One who deserves the glory. Jesus is the only One worthy of our praise. The rest of us are sinners. We miss the mark. Often.

While it's important to think positive and strive to be better people, we need to remember we're not going to be perfect in this life. Now, I'm not saying we use this truth as an excuse to purposely do stupid or wrong things and not accept responsibility when we miss our target. Of course not! I'm simply reminding us we are fallen in nature and we need to be sure our attention, our focus, and our gaze rest on Jesus alone. Not on ourselves and certainly not on others. Because the truth is, at some point and in some way, we're going to hurt someone's feelings. We're going to fall into temptation. We're going to get discouraged. We're going to feel like quitting. We're going to choose our feelings over what's right. This is why we need Jesus. Apart from God's grace, not one of us is whole or complete or righteous.

I remember the first time I visited a prison in the Philippines. My brother Peter and I, accompanied by a translator that we ended up not needing, shared the Good News of God to a little over fifty prisoners that day. When we arrived, I was pumped. Adrenaline coursed through my body along with a mixture of fear, stemming from being in an open room with murderers, rapists, and drug dealers, and excitement from having the opportunity to tell these men how much God loves them.

The building was narrow, long. Cells that housed five or six inmates each lined both sides of the corridor. Strange thing was, none of the cells had doors, so the prisoners could come and go as they pleased. As that ignited some fear, I quickly started spitting out in my mind the Bible verses I learned as a kid.

Peter and I positioned ourselves at the back of the building, facing the men. Some stayed in their bunks. Others spilled out into the hallway, curious. While Peter spoke, I sat on a stool next to him, looking up at my big brother, proud. As he neared the closing, Peter started tweaking his message. Explaining how Jesus loved us so much that He died for our sins, he said something that at first didn't sit well with me. Peter said, "*My* sins nailed Jesus to the cross."

Why did he say "my"? Peter's personalization of the gospel message threw me off. *He's my brother,* I thought, feeling conflicted. *It wasn't just his sins that nailed Jesus to the cross. I mean, c'mon. We're standing in the middle of a prison with people who committed a whole lot worse things than Peter did.*

And as my brother continued his talk, I started to cry. Right then, I felt God working in my heart, opening my eyes to the truth that I wasn't just a small part of the reason He died; I *was* the reason. However small and insignificant I as a teenager may have thought my sins were, they were significant enough to nail Jesus to the cross. Not only that, but in that moment I realized on a personal level that Jesus loved *me* so much that He died for *me*. And that even if I were the only person in the world, He still would have given His life so that I could be free from sin.

That experience made me look at grace in a new way. And it also made me realize that I am just as messed up and need Jesus just as badly as everyone else. I understood that I had no right to judge someone else for failing when I have fallen short myself. I needed to give grace to others in the same way it was given to me.

We have this tendency to idolize people, to think they're perfect or have a perfect life or a perfect marriage or a perfect body or a perfect family or a perfect job. Many of us see other people for what they choose to put out on Instagram or Facebook. The perfect selfie (that took fifteen shots and a few minutes of Photoshopping). The perfect picture with their spouse (that doesn't include a snapshot of the huge blowup they had the night before). The perfect record of the athlete on the field (that doesn't reflect his hardship in caring for a child with a life-threatening illness).

When we get caught up in these fake worlds, we can become disillusioned. We forget that each of us is human. Flawed. We all have bad thoughts. We all struggle with things. We all need grace. And we all need Jesus. Every. Single. One. Of us.

So instead of viewing those you admire as perfect and incapable of messing up and calling them out in judgment when they do, place your eyes on Jesus instead. He is perfect. He is the one constant who is forever doing right, forever loving, forever faithful, forever unchanging. Humans are flawed and limited, but God is not. We are human, He is not. Look up to God, not others.

And don't let the knowledge that you are an imperfect human being stop you from taking a stand. Think about what you can do to make life a little bit better, maybe even a little bit easier for someone else. Are you willing to volunteer for that organization? Or do the right thing at your job even though it's not convenient? Or fight for that child? Or commit to your family? Are you willing to take a stand for people in impoverished countries to have clean water? Or stand up for people who can't stand up for themselves?

What stand are you willing to take?

9

THE POWER OF DOING SOMETHING

Action is the foundational key to all success.

—PABLO PICASSO

've never heard from God. Audibly at least. No booming voice. No lightning bolt from the sky.

In my first book, *Through My Eyes,* I talked about the mental and emotional wrestling match I went through in deciding between playing for the Florida Gators and the Alabama Crimson Tide. I had solid relationships with both head coaches and admired them equally. Both schools were competitive and top-rated. I prayed and prayed. My family did the same.

By the time decision day rolled around, I didn't have an answer. How do you choose between something great and something just as great? The clock was ticking. Just minutes before ESPN started filming my college decision for the presentation of the Florida Dairy Farmers High School Player of the Year award, I still didn't know what I was going to say. Finally, when the mics were on and the cameras started rolling, I announced, "I will be playing college football next year at the University of Florida."

It seems many decisions I make involve the same type of grappling. Though I trust in God and aim to seek what He wants for my life, there are many times I get stuck not knowing what to do. Where do I live? Do I accept career offers to do things outside of being a quarterback in the NFL? Should I say yes to this speaking engagement or the other? Do I support this hospital, that child, this charity, or that business idea? The list is long.

Does my hesitancy in making a decision because I don't hear God tell me what to do make me a bad Christian? Of course not. It makes me human. And I'd prefer to err on the side of caution rather than say something like "God told me to do this or that." This has always sounded to me like pulling a trump card, the ultimate ace of spades. If God told me, who can argue with that? It is no small thing to speak for God.

I don't ever want to be responsible for the repercussions that follow making that statement and it not being true. I can't tell you how many times I've heard Christians throw those words around. At the time I was working on this book, in just one weekend of speaking at a few events, six people came up to me and said, "God told me that you are going to marry my daughter!" Interesting. God never told *me* that. And I've got a pretty big hunch that it is not God's will for me to have six wives!

This hearing-from-God stuff can be tricky. I definitely believe He speaks to people through a variety of ways. For starters, His voice is heard through the Bible. "All Scripture is inspired by God and profitable for teaching, for reproof, for correction, for training in righteousness."[1] I also believe we can hear Him through wise counsel, from those we trust. I can tell you that when I'm faced with a circumstance that warrants a tough decision, I pray long and hard, I try to listen to what I feel God puts on my heart, I seek wise counsel, and I reflect on my most important priorities. And then I am forced to make a decision.

Though I've never heard God's audible voice, I have felt drawn to notice certain people. Like Sherwin and his friends, like Robyn. I believe God works in my life this way. While He didn't tell me out loud to find Sherwin or to stop what I was doing to talk to Robyn, I feel like He moved my heart to pay attention to them.

I know how hard it can be when we hit a crossroad in life and are not sure what to do. Outside of God giving us crystal-clear, step-by-step instructions or guidance, it can be tempting to get stuck. We don't know which direction to travel in. When do we stay put? When do we move on? What job offer do we take? Whom do we marry? Do we expand our family? Where do we go to school? Should we start this ministry? And sometimes in the absence of hearing answers from God, we do nothing. Certainly there is a time to wait on God, but rarely is there a time to do absolutely nothing.

You know what happens when we do nothing? Nothing.

I've been talking about the importance of taking stands to impact others. This requires action. Playing video games or watching reality television all day is not going to encourage your neighbor or help someone who is struggling. Now, I'm not saying that playing Xbox or watching TV is bad; I'm just saying that if you are truly looking to make a difference, you have to start doing something that can make a difference. Don't let life get in the way of choosing to impact others. There is always something to do.

Pay attention.

Look around.

Listen.

God just might be speaking.

JUST SAY YES

Since I was a freshman in college, I've visited about twelve American prisons, many of them multiple times, sharing with inmates the love and hope of Jesus.

One of those visits came about when Jim Williams, who has been work-ing in prison ministry for more than forty-two years, offered Erik, Robby, and me the opportunity to join him in ministering to inmates on death row at Florida State Prison. It's one of the largest prisons in the state and the only one with an execution chamber. While I had visited there several times previ-ously, this was the first time my older brother Robby and my friend Erik came with me.

Though Robby had shared the Good News with inmates in prison in the Philippines, this was his first time doing so in the States, and he was real ex-cited. Erik was particularly anxious. He kept shooting us questions: "What is it like? Are the inmates dangerous? Will a guard be with us the whole time?" I empathized with the guy and kept reassuring him everything was going to be fine.

I remember my first time visiting a prison. Like Erik, I didn't know what to expect. As I stood in the yard of a maximum-security prison, bordered by a high fence, staring at the hardened faces of men doing time, some sporting teardrop tattoos, others swastikas, I felt overwhelmed. It was one thing to talk to men behind bars; it's another thing to stand in an open area with them, giving them hugs and shaking their hands. That can be pretty intimi-dating. I was also just a nineteen-year-old kid, and many of the men in the yard had years of life experience on me. My mind raced. *How am I going to do this? What am I going to say?*

I remembered a radio interview I had done recently. The host had asked if I would consider myself a success. I said yes, but not because of football; it was because I have a relationship with Jesus Christ. I told the men in that prison yard a slightly tweaked version of what I had told the radio host. I told them that I had a relationship with the God of the universe and that they could too. I told them that although some people on the outside may have forgotten about them, there was one man who never would—Jesus. The moment I started sharing the message on my heart, my nerves vanished. I closed my talk by extending an invitation. "If you want to trust Jesus," I said, "I'd love for you to stand up and stand right next to me." I'll never forget the big guy in the front row of the crowd, a hard-looking dude. I'd seen him before I started talking. Noticing how the other inmates interacted with him, I could just tell he had the respect of the masses. Imagine my surprise when he stood up and made his way beside me. Words can't express how grateful I was.

Fast-forward almost ten years. I was eager to see what God had in store for Robby and Erik.

The sky was overcast that day, matching the mood of the prison facilities. A steel sign welcomed us, stretching from one side of the roadway to the other, blaring in capital letters "Florida State Prison." A number of grim-looking concrete buildings sat on the property, surrounded by a high chain-link fence stacked with rows of razor-wire spirals. It looked intimidating, grisly. We walked into one of the buildings, the front area flanked by steel-faced guards. We prayed under our breath while waiting for the warden, a man I had met before and respect. A strong Christian, he's tough but loves the inmates and treats them with decency. I like that.

While we didn't get patted down, we did have to empty our pockets and go through a metal detector. After I took pictures with and signed autographs for the warden and fellow correctional officers, Jim, Robby, Erik, and I sat in a conference room listening to the warden give us detailed instructions on what to do and what not to do during our time visiting death row. I listened, but since I'd done this before, I was more attuned to the wall in front of me. From left to right, hung like trophies, were weapons that had been confiscated from the inmates. Clubs, knives, pipes, chains, hammers, pliers, and razor blades splattered the wall, the sharp edges menacing, the instruments powerful. I've often wondered how many of them claimed the life of another. I definitely don't think this wall helped calm Erik's building anxiety.

"Don't get too close," the warden reminded us. "Remember, these men are dangerous. You might think you're protected on the other side of the cell bars, but you'll be surprised what these inmates are capable of. Make sure you stand about an arm's length away from the cell. They could easily be holding a blade or sharp instrument in their hands."

In theory, this warning made sense. The closer you are, the more damage an inmate can potentially do. But I break this rule all the time. Though I'm not technically allowed to shake an inmate's hand, I do it anyway. Call me an old-fashioned southern boy, but it's the right thing to do. And yeah, there have been times my friendliness was not appreciated. I've had inmates try to break my hand in a handshake. Some have threatened to kill me. Some have tried to throw their feces on me. You never know what can happen visiting a prison. Many inmates have begged me to fight for their cases. I've seen violent fights break out in prison yards, inmates beating others within an inch of their lives. I've even met a guy who killed a bunch of people over a video game. Never a dull moment.

The warden continued, "Also, don't get into small talk, like the weather. Some of these guys have been stuck inside four walls for a while. They don't know whether it's sunny or cloudy, and they don't need to be reminded of that."

Jim, Robby, Erik, and I then walked into another building, passing through a labyrinth of barbed wire, concrete walls, and guarded gates. It seemed each passing step led us deeper into an abysmal dungeon. We couldn't carry anything with us other than our driver's licenses and the reading material we brought that shared God's message of love and hope (minus the staples the guards had pried off and thrown out).

On our way to the death-row area, we talked to other inmates. A few of them, familiar with college ball, started yelling my name and doing the Gator chomp. Another noticed and started talking smack in response, pledging allegiance to Miami. It's amazing how deep a rivalry in sports can run, even in prison. Something else struck me that day. I talked to a handful of men who had some sort of connection with me. One said he heard me speak at such-and-such event. One said he tackled me in some high-school game. Another said he had been to the church where I grew up. It was uncanny. Being inter-twined in these lives even in indirect ways made the experience more real.

After sharing a bit with these men, we continued our journey. The war-den led us down one of many long and dark hallways we would walk through that day. After passing a few stony-faced guards who nodded to us in greet-ing, we reached the final cellblock.

"This is a solemn place," the warden said quietly right before introducing us to a waiting gentleman, the death-watch commander. This man was re-sponsible for death-row inmates during their final days prior to their execu-tion. With a serious demeanor, he led us inside the death chamber. The room was dimly lit, cold. We stared, spines tingling, at the lethal-injection table. Though this wasn't my first time seeing it, it still gave me chills. Covered with multiple leather straps, it lay adjacent to a large window that faced into the witness room from where the execution could be watched. Standing omi-nously in another corner of the room was the electric chair, nicknamed Old Sparky. Sounds like a cute name, but trust me, there's nothing cute about it. The three-legged wooden contraption was outfitted with similar leather straps and fixed permanently to the ground. Besides the death-watch com-mander, none of us said a word. No doubt the room was creepy, the atmo-sphere heavy. You couldn't help but feel the weight of darkness around you.

Finally, a few hours after arriving at the prison, we were escorted to death row, listening while the warden gave us a few details of the crimes that had warranted these death sentences. One had killed a correctional officer. One had raped and murdered a twelve-year-old girl. Another killed three people in cold blood. Each inmate imprisoned within these tiny, three-walled concrete vaults had committed heinous crimes. Surprisingly, death row was quiet. The warden mentioned the noise level got worse at night, when the men wrestled with their demons in nightmares.

The first inmate I spoke to recognized me right away. "Hey," he called out in a friendly tone. "Why aren't you playing for the Jaguars?"

As I'd always done, I ignored the warden's warning and stepped right up to the bars of the cell and talked to the inmate, learning that he had read the Bible a few times and found it boring. I told this man that God loved him and had a plan for his life, even though it may not seem like it from behind bars. I shared with him the story of how Jesus was condemned to die alongside two other criminals, one of whom believed in Him. I shared how we've all sinned and fallen short, and that it's never too late to change our eternal fate. He listened respectfully but wasn't interested.

The four of us offered words of hope to these men, housed in six-by-nine-foot cells, where they spent twenty-three hours of each day. I noticed that Erik wasn't nervous anymore. Like Robby, through the power of the Holy Spirit, he was growing bold. We were each enveloped in the presence of peace. God was there, even in a place shadowed by despair and hopelessness. It's why we felt so comfortable standing only an inch or two away from some of the most violent criminals in the country.

One particular inmate mentioned he had played football at a high school near mine. We talked for a few minutes, him asking if I was happy because I had money, a nice house, or a hot chick, then me explaining that true joy comes from Jesus. Before we left, we celebrated his decision to accept the gift of grace that Jesus gives to all who believe. We gave him a Bible, writing on the inside flap "April 7, 2015. A new start." Robby grabbed the guy's hand through the steel bars and pulled him as close as he could in a man hug and said, "Welcome to the family!"

When it was time to go, I felt drained. There's something about being in a place where you can sense, even feel, the oppressing powers of darkness. It physically affects you, bears heavy on your soul. I literally felt like I'd been walking around with a weighted vest for hours. Sharing with inmates is a very emotional experience, filled with highs and lows. You talk to some guys who are excited to hear a message of hope and others who couldn't care less. The differences are extreme. So when I walked away from what I thought was the last cell of the day, my energy level was burned out. And as I walked back down a series of dark hallways, my footsteps echoing off the concrete walls, I caught a glimpse of light at the end of the corridor. A cue. I was ready to go home.

But instead of turning left toward the light, the warden asked if we would spend some time with the prison nurses in the medical ward; they had been going through a tough time, though I can't remember why specifically. We said yes, then made a right turn down another dark corridor. A half hour or more had passed when I noticed Erik looking around, curious. He pointed to a mystery hallway and asked the warden, "What's down there?"

I'm not proud to say this, but in that moment I groaned on the inside. *Oh man, we've been here forever.* It wasn't that I didn't want to talk to any more people, whether inmates or prison staff; I just felt emotionally depleted. I was running on empty.

"Ah," the warden replied in a hushed tone. "That's suicide watch."

"Are there any inmates?" Erik asked.

"Yes, four."

I felt God grabbing hold of my heart, pulling me toward that corridor. It was as if He was saying, "Timmy, you can wait to rest. There's something I want you to see." Feeling prompted to visit the men on suicide watch, I walked, not far, and stood in front of four side-by-side suicide-resistant cells.

Each cell had padded walls and a steel door with a small, cloudy Plexiglas window and, underneath, a slot where meals were served. Extreme measures are taken to make sure inmates don't commit suicide, so they are forced to wear what look like straitjackets and restraints on their ankles.

I approached the first cell. Because the door and walls were so thick, I had to press my face right against the murky glass and talk real loud. The first guy I shared with gave no response. His eyes were blank. I took a few steps over to the next cell, introduced myself, and started sharing. Same response. Nothing but a thousand-yard stare.

Before I approached the third cell, the warden grabbed my arm and whispered, "Tim, I think you should know something before you talk to this guy. He's in prison because he killed someone. But also, a few days ago, he killed another inmate. And now, he will do anything to kill himself."

I nodded, trying to process the man's desperate place, not knowing what to expect. As I grabbed a sip of water, the warden took a few steps ahead of me and pressed his face into the window of this third cell. "Hey, buddy. You have a special visitor you might want to come see."

I switched places with the warden and peered into the smudged Plexiglas. The view was blurry, but I could see a man, arms constricted by a straitjacket, shuffling his way toward me. As his face pressed against the glass, we locked eyes. Immediately, the man, who looked younger than me, gasped in shock, his mouth dropping to the floor. "You're a Christian!" he exclaimed. I hadn't seen this type of reaction from any of the other prisoners that day.

"Yes sir. I am. Do you know why we're here?"

"No."

"We're here to tell you that God loves you."

At some point Erik said, "I think that we are here specifically to tell you that."

When the young man heard these words, he crumpled to the floor like a rag doll, tears pouring down, his shoulders shaking in violent sobs.

I was speechless, watching a hardened criminal cry like a baby. It took a few minutes for him to compose himself. Unable to use his arms, he struggled to stand up and awkwardly stumbled his way back to the window.

"Let me tell you something," the man began, his voice strong, loud, filled with passion. "Let me tell you something. I prayed to that God for the first time in my life. I said, 'God, you ain't never been there for me and you ain't never done anything for me. Everything in my life has been hard. I've been neglected and I've been abandoned. No one's had my back. I have no hope. If you're real, show me something! If not, I'm going to do anything I can to kill myself!' And five minutes later"—he paused for a second, stifling a sob—"you guys show up." And then he broke down again, weeping. In that moment, this man came face to face with the fact that God answers prayer. And God had allowed us to be part of that answer.

I couldn't help but cry. God had a special plan for this young man. And even though at first I didn't feel like walking down suicide watch, even though I was emotionally exhausted, even though I was looking forward to the plans I'd made to go home with my friends, God had another plan in mind. And what mattered most was not how I felt, but that this man had an appointment to meet Jesus.

The four of us, splashed with tears of joy, prayed with this young man as he committed his life to God. When we were through, he looked like a different person. His face was softer, the hard edges gone. His smile was wide, bright. His eyes twinkled, full of life. New life.

Standing in a prison cell in suicide watch, shackled by chains, confined by a straitjacket, this man moved from darkness to light. Even though he will likely remain behind bars for the rest of his life, the truth has set him free.

THE TIME IS NOW

God wants us to be a part of awesome things, but we have to say yes to doing something. I'm challenging you in ways I've been challenged and am challenging myself. I'm a big believer of doing something when you feel like it, when you don't feel like it, when you're motivated, and when you're not. When you're faced with the opportunity to do the right thing, to better someone else's life, help lessen someone's struggle, or simply brighten someone's day, just do it.

There may be times where you will be drawn to someone to encourage or pray for, but there are plenty of times when that feeling isn't there. It's still just as important to do the right thing. We don't have to feel led into full-time ministry before we help the homeless or share a message of hope with someone who may need it. The only qualification necessary is willingness.

I know not everyone has the opportunity to visit hospitals or prisons or make wishes come true. But there is always something you can do, even when you're in a busy season in life. Give someone a hug. Send a text with an inspiring quote. Mail someone a heartfelt card. Donate blood. Tell someone how much you appreciate him or her.

If we open our eyes, each day presents us with opportunities to do something kind or nice for someone else. I've heard many people say that when they win the lottery, they're going to donate a ton of money to an orphanage, open a food bank, or quit their job and serve the poor. These are certainly admirable ambitions. But what are your chances of winning the lottery? Here's an interesting fact. You have one shot in almost fourteen million of picking the six winning numbers from forty-nine possible numbers. Buy a lottery ticket in this scenario every week and you may win once every 269,000 years.[2] In other words, don't count on it. So instead of waiting to strike it rich, do something now. You don't have to fork over your paycheck to save orphans. Support one for less than the price of a cup of coffee a day. Or volunteer for a local organization.

Don't wait for something to happen or for someone to give you permission to do something right. Just do it. When's the right time? For the most part, always.

One of my favorite sayings is "Oftentimes we don't dream big enough and oftentimes we don't start small enough." It makes me think of our annual Night to Shine event. In 2014 our foundation felt led to start this movement, a nationwide prom centered on God's love for people with special needs ages sixteen and up. Our goal was simple: find a way to work together with churches around the country to host proms to celebrate and love on these amazing people.

In just its second year, God has grown Night to Shine to more than two hundred churches representing twenty-three denominations in forty-eight states and seven countries. Over seventy thousand volunteers all over the world gave thirty-two thousand honored guests an amazing experience that culminated in all of them being crowned as the king or queen of the prom. The event offered volunteer opportunities around the world. Some volunteers acted as a buddy. Some simply stood on the red carpet and cheered. Some did hair and makeup. Some stood on a stage and emceed. Some shined shoes. Some parked cars. Some helped decorate. Some helped with the sound system. There was something for everyone to do.

Although events like this are great and provide tons of volunteer opportunities, you don't have to wait for a special event to serve someone. You can start right now. Look around. Do you know someone who might need some encouragement? Or see someone who might need a hand? Take a step of faith and do something for that person.

VANTAGE POINT

I remember years ago visiting with an eleven-year-old boy who had cancer, along with his family. Though I can't remember why, I was in an emotional slump, struggling through disappointment or some other powerful emotion. Not feeling particularly motivated, I headed off to spend time with these folks.

When I arrived at their home on a Sunday afternoon, the boy's parents greeted me warmly. We sat down and they shared their son's story. A malignant tumor had ruptured in and shattered his shoulder. A huge baseball fan and player at his school, he was unable to use his throwing arm anymore. The boy was heartbroken. Sadly, his mom told me that she, too, had been recently diagnosed with cancer. My bad day didn't seem so bad anymore. In fact, it seemed meaningless in the big picture. We prayed together for a bit before we walked into the boy's room, so he could show me his Gator shrine.

Within the first step I took inside this bedroom, I noticed it was decked out in Tim Tebow autographed memorabilia that his parents had purchased online or through eBay. None of it was authentic.

"I love your room, buddy," I said, smiling as I plopped down on the edge of his bed. The sweet kid with bedhead grinned from ear to ear.

"So," I started, looking all around the room, "I have good news and bad news. The bad news is that all these signed footballs and pictures and stuff are fake."

His eyes fell. "What? Are you kidding me?"

"But there's good news," I reassured him. "The good news is that I will make them all real, and quick!"

We talked for a while and prayed some. Our time together was powerful, uplifting. Spending time with this precious boy and his parents changed my perspective. It's interesting what happens when you do something in spite of your feelings. Many times, you walk away being blessed by the one you think you're going to bless.

Humbling.

I went through similar mental shifts when I was playing in the NFL. You know how competitive I am. Winning is everything. And while I trained hard, did my best, and wanted with everything in me to win, there were times I had to remind myself it was just a game. Not that it wasn't important, or that it wasn't a big deal, or that it didn't matter. But when millions of Americans are tuning in to watch you perform for the next three hours and the pressure of winning or losing starts to mount in an all-consuming way, you need perspective. I had to remind myself that I was just playing a game while many others are fighting for their lives.

I got a lot of flak for spending time with many W15H kids and others pre- and postgame. Some critics said it made me a distraction to the team and even made me distracted on the field. I disagree. I believe these kids helped keep my spirit in check. Though I performed just as competitively, most times keeping the right perspective allowed me to handle the pressures of winning and losing. Of not feeling like if I didn't score a touchdown, my life would be over.

Think about this. What was more important? Bringing a smile to someone's face—someone like Bailey Knaub, who to date has undergone seventy-five surgeries and numerous rounds of chemotherapy battling a rare disease with no known cause or cure—or scoring a touchdown?

Society doesn't get to define what's important in my life. Although I may not get a pat on the back or an attaboy from others, I'd rather have my heavenly Father be proud of me.

MY HEROES

One of the many ways these W15H kids and others I've met along the way have inspired me is how, in the midst of dealing with serious, even life-threatening illnesses, they help and love on others. They do something for someone else.

In my first book I talked about Kelly Faughnan, a vivacious young woman with a million-dollar smile. I met her in Orlando in 2009, and she agreed to be my date to the Home Depot College Awards.

Kelly was born with a hearing impairment and gross motor delays. When she was thirteen years old, she started to experience tremors in her right hand and arm. For the next few years, she was seen by countless specialists who were unable to pinpoint the problem and who prescribed a variety of anti-tremor medications, none of which worked. Eventually, the tremors began to affect her left arm and hand as well.

Six months after graduating high school, doctors at Johns Hopkins discovered a tumor on Kelly's brain stem. On one hand, the news was frightening. On the other, if that was the cause of the tremors and could be removed, the news offered a glimpse of hope. On December 15, 2008, Kelly underwent brain surgery. Despite the tumor being removed, the tremors continued. To date, no one has been able to diagnose Kelly's condition, let alone treat it.

Kelly is a force to be reckoned with. She is a positive and inspirational powerhouse who refuses to let a debilitating medical condition keep her from enjoying life and making a difference. Oh sure, she has bad days. Sometimes she is embarrassed by the tremors and the way others may perceive her because of them. And sometimes she is bothered by the fact that she struggles with the simplest of tasks that require fine motor skills, like using utensils, buttoning her clothes, or writing. But Kelly fights hard not to let these things bother her. She says with a smile, "My tremors are a part of me. I am the person God made me to be."

Instead of feeling sorry for herself, Kelly is reaching out to others. After we met for the first time, I stayed in contact with her, and two years later she received a W15H. Grateful for the experience, Kelly was inspired to do something herself. She started a golf tournament and an ice-cream-parlor raffle in her hometown and donated all the proceeds to my foundation. Kelly says, "The golf tournament is my way of using the blessings I have been given to create a brighter day in the lives of children who are facing challenges of their own." The event was so successful that Kelly has organized one every year. And to date, she has raised eighty-five thousand dollars.

Incredible!

I was a senior in college, playing my last year of football as a Gator when I met seven-year-old Boomer, an adorable kid with a mischievous smile. Boomer was born at twenty-eight weeks. When he was just over a year old, his mom, Brooke, noticed he wasn't progressing with typical milestones. A neurologist diagnosed Boomer with schizencephaly, a developmental birth defect, and cerebral palsy. Similar to Robyn (see chapter 7), Boomer has had multiple Botox injections, surgeries that have required him to wear body casts for months, and weekly physical therapy. He also lives with severe chronic pain. Despite these obstacles, he has defied doctors' initial predictions that he would never sit up, never walk, and not live past age five.

Boomer and his mom drove down to Florida from Atlanta to meet me for the first time before the Gators opened the season. I had a blast wheeling this incredible kid (and huge Gator fan) around the field for warmups before the game and in between the maze of benches in the locker room. We stayed in touch after that, sending each other encouraging texts. Boomer came to almost every home game that season. And this cool dude was there when I played my last game in college. I gave him the football as a keepsake as well as my last hug as a Gator on the field during the Sugar Bowl.

The first year we held the foundation's Celebrity Golf Classic, we did our best to fill the room with a bunch of supporters and donors who could help our cause. The logistics of planning was a daunting task—rallying celebrities to attend, planning minute-by-minute schedules, coordinating venue details, organizing the different events. Our staff was small and put in countless hours of work.

We launched the event with a prayer, led by none other than Boomer, who was accompanied by his mother. In a ballroom decked out with fancy tableware and chandeliers, this amazing kid, looking dapper in a three-piece suit and tie and exuding playful charm, rolled up to the front of the podium in his wheelchair. After he led the room in a moving opening prayer, he did something astonishing.

As Boomer left the stage, he handed me a clear Ziploc bag with a few crumpled dollar bills and a bunch of loose change, twenty-seven dollars in total. On the bag written in blue ink was "To Timmy's foundation, From Boomer."

"I saved this from my allowance," he said, beaming. "I want to help. I want to give it to you." I choked back a tear as I leaned down and took the plastic bag from him, the change jiggling wildly. Still on stage, I shared with all these wealthy and influential people Boomer's act of generosity, and immediately it struck a chord. The supporters of the foundation were in tears, moved by the inspiring gesture of a little boy who chose to do something. Boomer ignited a chain of benevolence from donors that night.

It's amazing to me how in the midst of our carefully laid-out plans, calculated objectives, and rigid schedules, God can work some magic.

Do something. Trust me, it counts.

The next year, Boomer surprised us again. This time, he sent letters out to family and friends in hopes of raising money for the foundation. In our second golf event, this amazing boy presented us with checks totaling $9,267. Every single person in that room started crying, as most had attended the gala the year before and remembered Boomer. It was a powerful and emotional moment, which led to more generosity. In fact, one supporter donated a thousand dollars in Boomer's name to total his donation over ten grand.

Many people don't even try to reach out and help others because they're scared their efforts won't matter or won't make much of a difference. Have courage and at least try. Even if you fail, at least you will have planted a seed. You don't know what God can do with one step forward, with a raised hand, with a heart that says yes, with five loaves and two fish, with a slingshot and a few stones. Don't limit what He can do based on how you limit yourself. Be yourself, and let God be God.

The little things we do each day add up to something greater, something we will ultimately leave behind. And what that ends up looking like for you and for me will depend on how we live, knowing whose we are.

10

WHAT MATTERS MOST

**There is so much more to our existence
than what we can see. What we do reverberates
through the heavens and into eternity.**

—Francis Chan

E leven seconds.

What can you do in eleven seconds? Wash your hands. Send a text. Tie your shoes. Google something. Download an app.

Meb Keflezighi won the 2014 Boston Marathon by eleven seconds.

And eleven seconds into overtime, the Denver Broncos knocked the Pittsburgh Steelers, the number one defense in the NFL at the time, out of the AFC playoffs, 29–23.

It was a chilly day in Denver, January 8, 2012. As I warmed up pregame, it was hard to shake the disappointment from losing the last three games against the Patriots, the Buffalo Bills, and the Kansas City Chiefs. The losses were painful, not to mention contradictory, considering the six-week winning streak we had celebrated before that. A string of unimaginable wins, including four fourth-quarter comebacks, against Oakland, Kansas City, the New York Jets, San Diego, Minnesota, and Chicago.

The media was eating the dichotomy up. After we lost 14–40 to Buffalo, Bill Maher took to Twitter with a profanity-laced blow against my faith. On Christmas Eve, no less. Others in the media asked where God was during our three-week slump.

My performance was no doubt less than stellar; during those last three games I only completed 41 percent of my passes. It was disheartening to see how some of the public blamed God for the losses. Hey, I never said He orchestrated our wins or executed our crazy comebacks; I just thanked Him in those moments. It's amazing how we can take things out of context.

So on that chilly January day, taking the field in practice, warming up with my fellow teammates prior to facing the Steelers, I felt a bit tense, struggling to set aside our three defeats. I reminded myself of the psalms I had been studying recently. Much of this collection of prayers and poems was written by David, a king of ancient Israel, the warrior boy who took out the giant. I've always loved reading them because they depict so intimately the human struggle in living a life of faith. In these psalms, David put words to a wide spectrum of his emotions. In one he writes how thankful he is for God, His provision, and for always having his back. In the next he bemoans the fact that his enemies, which over the years included his own son and a former mentor, the then-reigning king of Israel, are pursuing him relentlessly. And in another, we read how David is at peace in the midst of his shaken world, settled in his spirit, knowing that even when life isn't easy, God is still with him. Frankly, it's the most honest piece of journaling I've ever read.

That day I brought to mind Psalm 16:8: "I have set the LORD continually before me; because He is at my right hand, I will not be shaken." I remembered when I was a sophomore in high school, quarterback of our football team. Every Friday night before games, my parents would always encourage me with Bible verses, using examples to make them practical in real life. After my mom read Psalm 16:8 to me, I asked her for a black

Sharpie. Then, I scribbled something on my hand. Mom assumed I was writing down a play or something.

After we won the game, she asked, "Honey, what did you write on your hand?" I opened my palm with a smile. Though the mixture of sweat and dirt had smudged some of the letters, on my right hand, in faint black, was the word *God*.

That afternoon in Denver, I soaked my spirit in Psalm 16:8, remembering He was at my right hand. I made a choice to praise and thank God. I would have loved a win, of course, but regardless of the outcome, I made the choice to keep trusting and keep thanking my heavenly Father.

Imagine my surprise during the pregame warmup when familiar faces showed up on the field. My good friends Gary, Joe Don, and Jay, who happen to make up one of my favorite bands, Rascal Flatts, surprised me. I hadn't a clue they were coming and later learned my brother Robby had made it happen. It was especially surprising because Gary and his family had stayed at my house the weekend before. That day, before we Broncos faced the Steelers, Gary, Joe Don, Jay, and I had a blast playing catch on the field. And hearing these talented guys sing the national anthem a few hours later filled my heart with such gratitude, not to mention my entire family's, who had come to support me on the sidelines.

Gary, Joe Don, Jay, and my family weren't the only ones who spent time with me pregame. I was honored to be able to hang out with Bailey, one of our W15H kids I mentioned in the last chapter. Diagnosed with a rare disease that forms tumors in her face, lungs, and kidneys, Bailey's had seventy-five surgeries to date and has lost a lung in the process. Despite her medical battle, this girl is on fire. I'll never forget how encouraging she was to me. As the stadium started filling with football fans, she, in her inimitable calming way, told me, "Relax, Timmy! I'm praying for you. You're going to do awesome!"

It's amazing to me how Bailey helped put the game into perspective. While I had felt weighed down by the pressure to win this big game against the best defense in the NFL, this young woman brought me a sense of calm. And by the time our team lined up on the opening snap and seventy-six thousand football fans started screaming, I was ready.

The first quarter was lackluster, our Broncos offense managing only eight yards, with no passes completed on my part. But in the second quarter, we pulled the trigger. After hitting Eric Decker and Demaryius Thomas on a few big plays, we got the ball rolling. By the time we huddled in the locker room during halftime, the Broncos were up 20–6.

Our lead didn't last long. The Steelers came on strong in the second half, scoring on three straight possessions. And with 3:48 remaining in the game, the Steelers knotted the score 23–23 with a thirty-one-yard touchdown pass. The game ended in a tie.

Pittsburgh called tails for the overtime coin toss. The shiny penny (or whatever it was) landed heads up on the grass.

I didn't know how long it would take, but I knew the play we'd make. We talked about it on the sidelines. And in watching how the Steelers had played the game, it seemed a perfect fit. Their team had an aggressive defense and had been trying to stop our zone-read. This one play, I thought, just might be our golden ticket.

After the refs explained the NFL's new overtime rules, one of which stated that a touchdown on the first possession would constitute a victory, we set up on the twenty. When the ball snapped, my confidence grew. *We might have a chance with this play.* When Thomas did a great job getting inside the corner, crossing in front of the safety, I knew we definitely had a chance.

I faked to halfback Willis McGahee and threw to a streaking Thomas. As we hoped, the Steelers overreacted on the play and gave Thomas the room he needed to catch the pass and take off down the sideline. Past the fifty. To the forty. Past the thirty. To the twenty, with Steelers safety Ryan Mundy chasing behind, his arms outstretched trying to grab Thomas as he whizzed forward like a speeding bullet. And eleven seconds after the ball was snapped, touchdown!

Mile High Stadium was delirious. Broncos fans jumped up and down like kids, whooping and hollering, while Steelers fans slowly disappeared from the bleachers one by one. This eleven-second play, to date known as the fastest overtime win in the history of the NFL, invited bedlam across the field. Swept up in the pandemonium, I took a knee, said a prayer, gave a mile-high salute, and celebrated with my teammates on the gridiron. Drowning in a sea of blue and orange, we hugged and high-fived, practically falling all over one another. The scene was surreal, the air punched with adrenaline and the sweet taste of victory. It's a moment I'll never forget.

This was the same game our PR guy said I threw for 316 yards, my yards per completion was 31.6, the time of possession was 31:06, the ratings were 31.6 million. And during the game ninety million people Googled "John 3:16"!

That day is one of the most memorable moments in my life. And while I appreciate the record-breaking scene as a highlight in my career, I know records are made to be broken. There will always be someone else to clinch next year's title, award, or trophy. These things don't last.

I want my life to speak louder than a world record. I don't just want to leave a legacy on the field. I want to live off the field in a way that outlives me. I want my love for God and for others to shine greater than an incredible comeback moment, a heavy gold trophy, or a handful of favorable headlines.

A few months after I won the Heisman in my sophomore year of college, I was invited to Thailand to speak to hundreds of missionaries serving in

South Asia, including my sister Christy and her husband Joey, who had moved to the region to serve. As I flew overseas, excited about the opportunity, I was also pretty nerve-racked. What was a twenty-year-old college kid going to share with a bunch of missionaries who were risking their very lives for the message of Jesus? Thoughts bombarded my head. *I'm not a theologian. I didn't even go to Bible school. I certainly don't have the kind of experience my dad does. And I haven't done anything as important as my sister and her husband.*

I wondered why I was even asked to speak. These missionaries were heroes, sacrificing so much in return for so little. They could teach me a thing or two. At the time, I was getting a lot of publicity as a college ballplayer, especially after winning the Heisman. I stared out the window of the plane as it flew over the Pacific Ocean. The sky beamed blue, the sun blasting my eyes. I imagined if I lived in a world that didn't have football, who would I be? Would I still matter? The more I struggled in trying to figure out what to share, the smaller and more insignificant I felt. Then, I felt God bring to my mind one of the Bible verses my parents forced me to memorize when trying to instill humility in my character.

> But the greatest among you shall be your servant. Whoever exalts himself shall be humbled; and whoever humbles himself shall be exalted. (Matthew 23:11–12)

Later, after I stepped down on Thai soil, I stood before hundreds of men and women—of different races, some older, some younger—and encouraged them from my heart. Using this verse, I told them that while some might look at movie stars or politicians or athletes as heroes, the real heroes are those who are humble. And because they had chosen to humble themselves and serve those some may consider "the least of these," God esteems them. As I concluded my talk, I told them that if the world could see them through God's eyes, they would be the ones winning the Heisman, not me.

I admire missionaries like Dad, Mom, Christy, and Joey, because they are intentionally investing in others in ways that will last for eternity. Now, we don't have to become missionaries to do this, but we do need to be purposeful in how we live our lives.

A LEGACY THAT LASTS

When I was younger, I read a poem written by Linda Ellis called "The Dash." She talks about the significance of the line separating the year of a person's birth and the year of the person's death. It's a simple little dash. Nothing fancy. Nothing big. This tiny mark of punctuation represents what we stand for, what or whom we impact, and ultimately what legacy we leave behind.

Think about your life. What mark are you leaving behind? How do you want your life to matter? I love what the authors of *A Leader's Legacy* wrote: "By asking ourselves how we want to be remembered, we plant the seeds for living our lives as if we matter."[1]

Think about the legacy you are building right now. Are you cultivating a life of generosity? Kindness? Compassion? Are you investing in others? Are your thoughts, your ideas, or your words implanted in the minds of others? Have you shared your failings with someone so he or she can learn from your mistakes? Have you motivated others with your story? Inspired someone through your song? Loved your children well?

If you look back on your life, do you wish you had worked more? Eaten more dessert? Taken more classes? Bought that car? Or do you wish you had spent time with the ones you love, showing others that they matter?

Not many of us want to think about our mortality. We prefer to distract ourselves instead. We watch mindless TV shows, overstuff our calendars, indulge in hobbies, and entertain ourselves into oblivion to take our minds off the fact that we won't be on this earth forever. We like to live like we're invincible. But ignoring the reality that our days are numbered may leave the most important questions in life unconsidered and unanswered.

When we think about our dash, we can live with more passion. We can identify our priorities. We can be intentional in how we live. We can make a difference and do things that matter. We can make choices that might be hard but are definitely worth it. We can take a stand for something, knowing its impact can be far-reaching and can leave a mark beyond our lives.

THE DIFFERENCE ONE CHOICE CAN MAKE

A few years back I spoke at an event where I shared the message of God's hope and love with thousands of people. After I ended my message, the emcee took over to close. I started walking toward the side of the stage as he thanked everyone for coming and the crowd broke out in final applause. I didn't get too far before I heard a loud female voice calling my name. I turned to the audience that was starting to pack up and leave and noticed a young woman in her twenties, tears streaming down her face, sprinting toward me. I wasn't the only one who saw her. Part of the event security team was nearby. One rushed to block me with his huge arms and another made a pass toward the woman, trying to keep her from getting too close. Undeterred by the security guard in front of her, she kept trying to move in my direction.

Suddenly, an older woman, just as emotional, rushed toward the young woman. She was holding a baby in her arms. Curious to see what the commotion was about, I took a few steps toward these two women. Security did the same. The older woman handed the baby off to the younger one, who was still calling out my name. She took the child and lifted her high in the air, above the head of the security guard in front of her. At this point, feeling both concerned for the woman and intrigued, I motioned for security to back off a bit so I could talk to her.

The young lady seemed relieved. Breathless, with a fresh flow of tears, she managed to sputter in between sniffles and sobs, "I just want you to hold a life that you helped save." Then she mentioned the TV commercial my mom and I had recently done in 2010. The message of the thirty-second clip was simple: Celebrate family. Celebrate life.

This young woman went to the website that shared my mom's story. She learned that when my mom became pregnant with me in the Philippines, she was very sick. The best doctor where they lived said that I was a tumor and advised my mom to abort me in order to save her life. She refused, trusting God with the outcome of my life and hers. While she was physically ill the entire time she was pregnant with me, her faith was strong. Mom was confident God was in control. You know how that story ends.

Years later, sitting with this young woman in an auditorium, I listened as she said, "A few days after the commercial aired, I was scheduled to have an abortion." Tears streamed down her face as she looked lovingly at her little girl. "But I didn't."

What a powerful moment. I can remember the handful of people who discouraged me from participating in the commercial. Many folks told me it was a bad idea and would sway certain sponsors to back out of their endorsement deals. But because I am passionate about celebrating life, I thought the commercial was brilliant. And I was honored to be a part of it. I believe that every life matters. No matter how big or little, no matter the race or nationality, no matter the disability or not, no matter if it's in the womb or fixing to go into the grave, every single life counts.

I admire Mom more than words can say for the legacy she is leaving us, a legacy of courage, of standing strong, and of always doing the right thing. It is my hope that one day my own children will say the same of me.

YOUR LIFE ECHOES

In the opening battle scene of the movie *Gladiator,* the Roman general Maximus (played by Russell Crowe), outfitted in battle gear, his suit of armor clanking with each stride, mounts a majestic horse and rides through thousands of troops that have spread out, prepared to battle. As he passes, the soldiers rise in respect and honor, ready to fight. Just prior to his giving the command to unleash hell, Maximus rallies the soldiers. In a short but moving speech, he reminds the men who fight for him, "What we do in life echoes in eternity."

I love these words. They're powerful, provocative. Think about the echoes that sound in your life right now. Where are you investing your resources? How are you spending your time? Your money? Your talents? How are you leveraging for a greater purpose the person God created you to be? Are you impacting others through your kindness, your courage, your compassion? Are you sharing hope? Are you living a life of love? Are you taking a stand? Doing something that matters?

Not long ago, I was in the process of reevaluating my goals and what I want to accomplish. Marker in hand, I stood in front of a giant whiteboard and started writing. In this brainstorming session, I noticed a recurring theme. That day I realized that my number one goal in life is to show Jesus through the way I live and the way I love. This doesn't mean I always do it right or the best way, but it's something I strive for.

I love 2 Corinthians 4:17–18: "Our light and momentary troubles are achieving for us an eternal glory that far outweighs them all. So we fix our eyes not on what is seen, but on what is unseen, since what is seen is temporary, but what is unseen is eternal" (NIV). Trophies don't last. Awards come and go. Impressive titles move from one person to the next. But how we live can make an eternal impact.

For the last two-plus years, I've been friends with a girl named Ansley Jones. I met her at Wolfson Children's Hospital in November 2013. This sweet and strong, then fourteen-year-old girl was diagnosed with leukemia a month before and was going through chemotherapy treatment. Ansley, whom I call "my southern girl" and who happens to be the nicest Georgia Bulldogs fan, is one of the most positive people I know. Despite being sick, she is full of joy, always smiling, laughing, and making jokes. Ansley has a way of making others light up. In fact, she's known for visiting with other kids in the hospital who are just as sick as she is to encourage them in the midst of their pain.

Through the foundation, we granted her a W15H and flew her and her family to Atlanta for the SEC Championship in December 2014. She enjoyed shopping at some of her favorite stores and visiting Topgolf and *SEC Nation*. We spent hours together that weekend, laughing and talking and dining on some of her favorite foods, like mouth-watering lobster (well, she ate it; I stay away from shellfish as a few folks in my family are allergic to it). Ansley's uplifting spirit continued to blow me away. She is truly an ambassador for faith, hope, and love, inspiring and encouraging everyone she meets, me included!

Two years after Ansley's initial diagnosis, the leukemia came back. As I was working on this book, she was in the hospital recovering from a bone-marrow transplant she had received from her brother, who thankfully was a perfect match. Every time I visited her, I'd sit next to her and we'd talk, pray, and have a blast creating a ton of Dubsmash videos with songs like "A Whole New World" and the soundtrack from *Grease*. Ansley is a tough cookie. One minute, overwhelmed by pain and sickness, she'd run to the bathroom to throw up, and in the next, she'd be smiling and laughing as if nothing had happened.

Ansley takes kindness to a whole new level. No matter how sick or tired she is, she is always so thoughtful and nice to everyone around her. Frankly, she makes me want to treat people better. It's easy to be kind to others when you're feeling great, but it takes resilience to do it when you're not feeling so hot. Ansley's life echoes to many people, me especially, through her courage to fight and her gracious spirit.

Think about your dash. Are you living in a way that is centered on yourself? Or are you, like Ansley, leaving a legacy that is going to make a difference in the lives of others for generations to come?

WELL DONE

A poet once said it right: "Only one life, / 'Twill soon be past; / Only what's done / for Christ will last."[2] I've talked a lot about investing in others because it's a big part of our identity in Jesus. When we know whose we are, we live differently. We are no longer the same. Our outlook changes. Our perspective shifts. We understand that some things we do on earth will last for eternity.

I've said in this book that while I appreciate the applause or pats on the back from others, what I really want to hear is my heavenly Father tell me, "I'm proud of you, son." This is my contemporary translation of the Bible's "Well done, my good and faithful servant."[3]

You know that John 3:16 is the essence of Christianity, depicting the heart of God who loved the world so much that He willingly sacrificed His only Son, Jesus, so that we could be free from the bondage of sin and live an abundant life.

Sin is not an easy word for many people to swallow. Put in simple terms, it means "missing the mark." We've all missed the mark. And even after inviting Jesus into our hearts, we continue to do so. Sin is what separates us from our heavenly Father. And no matter how many good deeds we rack up, no matter how kind we are to strangers, no matter how many homeless people we shelter, no matter how many orphans we help, no matter how many sick people we encourage, it will never be enough to reconcile us to God.

We can't bribe Him with our good works. Instead, we depend on what God did for us. He sent His Son, Jesus, to live on this earth, to die at the hands of those He came to love, and to break the chains of death through His resurrection. This is the Good News. In fact, it's the best news.

The ultimate legacy we can leave is a life of faith, believing the gospel and living in a way that exemplifies Jesus.

Two thousand years ago, a baby was born who would change the course of humanity. The Son of God left the perfection of heaven, a perfect relationship with the Father God, to come down to earth to die for the sins of the world. Jesus left it all for me. For you.

Looking at the scene from a human perspective, it's hard to believe. A simple teenage girl is chosen to carry the Savior of mankind. Nine months pregnant, tired, still trying to piece together the miracle in her belly, she simultaneously battles the fear of this task and cradles the wonder of the phenomenon. And she gives birth to the Son of God. In a barn. On a dirt floor caked with mud, scattered with rough straws of hay that bleating sheep and mooing cows trample on. The scene isn't pretty. It's not a delivery room with a soft bed, clean sheets, and the expert guidance of doctors and nurses. It's messy. It's unlikely. It's not how one would imagine the entrance of God into this world, what Christianity calls the Incarnation. It's ordinary. Without fanfare. Without paparazzi. Without flowers, balloons, and well wishes. God takes on human flesh. The Author of life enters our story.

And for thirty-three years, Jesus walks with humankind. Taking His first steps while His parents clap their hands in delight. Skipping stones on lakes. Horsing around with the neighborhood kids. As He grows up, Jesus works alongside His dad, a carpenter. And the same hands created to heal the lame and make the blind see chisel and sand slabs of oak into kitchen tables.

At just the right time, Jesus begins His public ministry. He gets baptized, igniting a three-year run reaching and teaching those who would listen. People flock to Him, drawn to His powerful yet mysterious words, His gentle yet commanding spirit. Men and women alike are captivated by the way He looks into their eyes, drawing deep into their souls, knowing what lies in the depths and still showing mercy. He heals people. He offers peace for their longings, living water for their thirst, forgiveness for their wrongs.

The religious elite of the day hate Jesus. They are infuriated by His claims to be the Son of God and the Son of Man, the Messiah. And ultimately, they plot to kill Him. Betrayed by one of His own followers, Jesus is arrested. Sentenced to die. And in one of the most excruciating forms of capital punishment, He is crucified on a wooden cross. Nails pierce through His hands and His feet. A crown of thorns presses into His skull.

Jesus is hung like dead meat next to two criminals. One curses Him, demanding that if Jesus is who He says He is, He should get them out of this mess. The other begs for mercy. And as that man takes one of his final breaths, Jesus promises him eternal life: "Today you shall be with Me in Paradise."[4] It's the pictorial definition of Romans 5:8, which says, "God demonstrates his own love toward us, in that while we were yet sinners, Christ died for us." When Jesus died for us, the weight of sin was upon Him. My sin. And your sin. And during that time, He experienced not just a physical death but the spiritual death of being separated from God the Father. Jesus was forsaken so we don't have to be. Jesus was abandoned so we don't have to be. God turned His back on Jesus, His Son, so He wouldn't have to turn His back on us.

What people planned for evil, God planned for good. While Jesus dies on the cross, an unseen cosmic transaction unfolds. Jesus takes on the punishment for our sins, and at the same time, His righteousness, and new life, become available to us. Through His death, He abolished the barrier that separates us from God. Instead of being alienated from our Creator, we can actually have a relationship with Him. We have the opportunity to be reconciled with God, forgiven of our sins, adopted into His family, and to receive an eternal home in heaven. This is a free gift. We can't earn it, and our best efforts will never be enough to deserve it. We only need to receive it by trusting Jesus.

On the third day after Jesus was crucified, He rose from the dead. The Christian faith is meaningless without this fact. Former atheist turned apologist C. S. Lewis wrote that Jesus "has forced open a door that has been locked since the death of the first man. He has met, fought, and beaten the King of Death. Everything is different because He has done so. This is the beginning of the New Creation: a new chapter in cosmic history has opened."[5]

I love what author Josh McDowell wrote: "No matter how devastating our struggles, disappointments, and troubles are, they are only temporary. No matter what happens to you, no matter the depth of tragedy or pain you face, no matter how death stalks you and your loved ones, the resurrection promises you a future of immeasurable good."[6]

When I think about leaving a legacy, I think about living in light of eternity. I think about basing my daily decisions on the future God has promised. I believe the greatest legacy we can leave is a life lived for Jesus. That starts with the most important decision you will ever make: the decision to trust Him. This is the best decision I ever made.

If you haven't done this yet, I want to encourage you to do it today. Right now, even.

You can express that trust in Jesus directly to Him in prayer. You can use my words below or use your own:

Dear Jesus, I know I am a sinner and need a Savior. Thank You that You died on the cross for me and rose again. I open the door of my heart and ask You to come in. I trust only You, Jesus. Thank You for coming into my heart and forgiving my sins. Thank You that God is my Father and I am His child. Thank You that I have a home in heaven and that I will come and live with You some day. In Your name, amen.

If you just prayed that prayer and put your trust in Jesus, several things took place. Your sins were forgiven, He now lives in you, you were adopted into God's family as one of His children, and you have the free gift of eternal life. Because this life you have in Jesus is eternal, He will never leave you. Jesus promised, "I will never leave you or forsake you."[7] Therefore you don't have to keep praying the above prayer over and over again. It's a permanent transaction between you and God. Think of it this way: after a guy gets married, he does not have to keep asking his wife to marry him again; they are already married.

If your world is shaken and you feel lost and heartbroken in your pain, accept God's gift of salvation. He offers you a new life, an abundant life. A life in union with Him. A life of meaning. A life of purpose. A life of joy. Yes, even in the midst of suffering.

The journey of faith isn't easy. Life isn't easy. But when you are united to Jesus by faith, you can begin to move mountains. Listen, you're going to doubt. You're going to fall short. You're going to struggle on some days. But know that God loves you. Know that He has an amazing plan for your life.

Trusting Him isn't a magic-carpet ride into a life free of problems, trouble, or suffering, but I can tell you that it's worth it. When you make the choice to show up and show out for Jesus, He will show up and show out for you.

I don't know what you are staring in the face at this very moment. Maybe you're struggling with finances, health, or relationships, or you feel like you just don't matter. Know this: Your past doesn't define you. Your circumstances don't define you. From this day forward, let God define whose you are. You can be a child of God.

Roy Lessin said, "Just think, you're here not by chance, but by God's choosing. His hand formed you and made you the person you are. He compares you to no one else—you are one of a kind. You lack nothing that His grace can't give you. He has allowed you to be here at this time in history to fulfill His special purpose for this generation."[8]

Continue to fight. Continue to hope. Continue to have faith.

I promise you, it's worth it.

Acknowledgments

Dad, you are the greatest man I know, with unmatched passion and courage. Through your devotion, commitment, and obedience to the Great Commission, you have changed countless lives for Jesus. Thank you for setting the example.

Mom, thank you! For everything! For giving me a chance, for always believing in me and my siblings, for pouring God's Word into our lives, for always wanting what's best for us, and for helping so many women all over the world along the way. If we've achieved anything, you're the reason why.

Christy, you're the best role model. Your wisdom and discernment has been such a blessing to me, especially through our late-night talks. Being able to watch you live out your faith in the highs and lows has been a true inspiration. Thank you for always being there for me.

Joey, you have blessed our family in more ways than you can imagine. Thank you for all the godly wisdom you've offered on this project and over the years, and for taking care of my sister. You're more than a brother-in-law; you are my brother.

Katie, you are a pillar of courage and inspiration. Thank you for how much you care, and for always putting a smile on my face. You bring so much life and spirit into my life and everyone around you. It's never a party if you're not there.

Robby, thank you for sticking by my side through thick and thin and for always having my back. We've been through a lot of highs and lows together, and there's no one else I'd rather have been with. You can have my rookie of DiMaggio.

Peter, I've always loved your heart and your tenacity. You're a fighter, and when you set your mind to something, nothing can stop you. I've loved watching you grow from brother to husband to father. Little Jackson is blessed to have you and Casey as parents!

Kevin, thank you for always being loyal and for being there for me since we were four years old.

Bryan, you know you're family and you'll always be. I'm excited to continue to do life with you.

Brad, thank you for bringing so much joy into my life. I'm so proud of what God is doing in yours.

Erik, thank you for being a great Christian brother and for the leadership and vision you have brought to the Tim Tebow Foundation.

To the staff and volunteers of TTF, thank you for the passion and dedication you bring to OUR foundation and the children we serve around the world.

To all the families and children we serve through TTF, thank you for allowing me to be part of your life! You have encouraged and inspired me by your amazing lives and stories.

Wendy, you are so much more than my attorney; you are family. Thank you for everything.

Annie, thank you for making the ship run smoothly—and always with a smile.

Ian, thank you for your friendship and wisdom.

To the Miller family, thanks for being my home away from home.

AJ, you crushed it! From your incredible patience, talent, and class, to your love of the Lord, I wouldn't want anyone else helping me share my story.

The Fedd Agency: Whitney and Esther, thank you for believing in this project and for your tireless devotion.

The team at WaterBrook (Tina, Alex, Laura B., Bruce, Laura W.): thank you for the insight and support you lent to this project.

To everyone who has ever prayed for me, thank you.

Notes

Chapter 2: Who Am I?

1. "The Unconditional Love of God," www.biblestudytools.com, September 13, 2012, www.biblestudytools.com/bible-study/topical-studies/the-unconditional-love-of-god.html.

2. 1 John 4:16.

3. See 1 John 4:8.

4. "The Unconditional Love of God."

5. Henri Nouwen, *The Inner Voice of Love: A Journey Through Anguish to Freedom* (New York: Image Books, 1998), 70.

6. Audio Adrenaline, *Hands and Feet* (Regal, 2007), back copy.

7. "Among Jordan's Great Games, This Was It," *Los Angeles Times*, March 29, 1990, http://articles.latimes.com/1990-03-29/sports/sp-582_1_michael-jordan.

8. Tim Keller, "The Wounded Spirit" (sermon, Manhattan, NY, December 5, 2004), http://verticallivingministries.com/2014/01/08/tim-keller-on-the-wounded-spirit-proverbs-series.

9. Ravi Zacharias, "Antidote to Poison," *Christianity Today*, April 26, 2013, www.christianitytoday.com/ct/2013/april/antidote-to-poison.html.

10. See John 6:5.

11. John 6:9, NLT.

12. See John 6:10, NLT.

13. Stephen Covey, *The 3rd Alternative: Solving Life's Most Difficult Problems* (New York: Free Press, 2011), 416.

Chapter 3: Facing the Giants

1. "Tim Tebow Leads 2-TD Rally as Broncos Stun Winless Dolphins in OT," ESPN.com News Service, October 24, 2011, http://espn.go .com/nfl/recap?gameId=311023015; Gray Caldwell, "The Comeback," Denver Broncos, October 23, 2011, www.denverbroncos.com/news -and-blogs/article-1/The-Comeback/cf2a853e-75d2-49ef-a497-b934 4631cb92.

2. "5368. phileó," Bible Hub, http://biblehub.com/greek/5368.htm.

3. David Nelmes, "God Is Agape Love," Ezilon Infobase, November 10, 2007, www.ezilon.com/articles/articles/7675/1/God-is-Agape -Love.

4. Luke 22:42.

5. Luke 22:44.

6. Luke 22:42.

7. USA Today Network, "North Texas 20-Year-Old Fights for Life Against Cancer," WFAA, September 6, 2014, www.cincinnati.com /story/news/state/2014/09/06/north-texas-20-year-old-fights-for -life-against-cancer/15209841.

8. See 2 Timothy 4:7, NIV.

9. Hebrews 11:1.

10. Martin Luther King Jr., quoted in Joseph Demakis, *The Ultimate Book of Quotations* (Charleston, SC: CreateSpace, 2012), 142.

11. "David and Goliath," All About the Bible, www.allaboutthebible.net /warfare/david-and-goliath.

12. 1 Samuel 17:8–9.

13. See 1 Samuel 17:18.

14. See 1 Samuel 17:20–26.

15. 1 Samuel 17:43.

16. 1 Samuel 17:45–46, NIV.

Chapter 4: The Voices of Negativity

1. Mark Kiszla, "Broncos Need New Meaning for Tim Tebowing," *Denver Post,* October 30, 2011, www.denverpost.com/broncos /ci_19228711.

2. Bruce Arthur, "Tebowing Mocking Enters Dangerous Territory," *National Post,* November 2, 2011, http://news.nationalpost.com /sports/nfl/tim-tebow-mocking-enters-dangerous-territory.

3. Sinclair Ferguson, *The Whole Christ: Legalism, Antinomianism, and Gospel Assurance—Why the Marrow Controversy Still Matters* (Wheaton, IL: Crossway, 2016), 154, italics in the original.

4. Ewald Plass, *Luther: A Character Study* (St. Louis: Concordia, 1948), 169.

Chapter 5: God's Got It

1. "Eagles Release QB Tim Tebow," ESPN.com News Service, September 6, 2015, http://espn.go.com/nfl/story/_/id/13588372/tim-tebow -released-philadelphia-eagles.

2. Job 1:8, MSG.

3. See Job 1:9–10.

4. See Job 1:11.

5. See Job 2:9.

6. Job 13:15.

7. See Job 38–39.

8. John 16:33, NLT.

9. Lloyd Sowers, "Teen's Death Gives Transplant Miracle to Florida Family," Fox 13, February 9, 2016, www.fox13news.com/news /local-news/87684957-story.

10. Gary White, "Mulberry Teen Gets a Second Heart Transplant," *Ledger* (Lakeland, FL), March 12, 2013, www.theledger.com/article/20130312 /NEWS/130319797?p=2&tc=pg.

11. Sowers, "Teen's Death."

12. See Hebrews 13:5.

13. Romans 8:28.

14. 1 Corinthians 13:12.

15. Lee Strobel, *God's Outrageous Claims: Discover What They Mean for You* (Grand Rapids, MI: Zondervan, 1997), 13.

16. This quote and variations on it have been attributed to multiple sources.

Chapter 6: The Others

1. Ecclesiastes 4:12.

2. Proverbs 18:24.

3. David DiSalvo, "Study: Helping Others Even in Small Ways Takes the Edge off Daily Stress," *Forbes,* December 21, 2015, www.forbes.com /sites/daviddisalvo/2015/12/21/helping-others-even-in-small-ways -takes-the-edge-off-daily-stress/#2a0b9aa35136.

4. DiSalvo, "Study: Helping Others."

5. Blago Kirov, *Ralph Waldo Emerson: Quotes and Facts,* Kindle ed. (2016), 303.

Chapter 7: Who Said Normal Is the Goal?

1. "What Is Cerebral Palsy?" www.shakeitoff4cp.com/wp-content /uploads/What-is-CP.pdf.

2. Psalm 139:13–18.

3. 1 Peter 4:10.

4. 1 Corinthians 4:7.

Chapter 8: Stand Up

1. Gary Langer, "Poll: Most Americans Say They're Christian," ABC News, http://abcnews.go.com/US/story?id=90356&page=1.

2. "Tebowing Accepted into English Language," Global Language Monitor, December 12, 2011, www.languagemonitor.com/new-words /tebowing-accepted-into-english-language.

3. See http://tebowing.com/about.

4. Simon Paige, *The Very Best of Winston Churchill: Quotes from a British Legend* (CreateSpace, 2014), 15.

Chapter 9: The Power of Doing Something

1. 2 Timothy 3:16.

2. "What Are Your Odds of Winning the Lottery?" Wonderopolis, http:// wonderopolis.org/wonder/what-are-your-odds-of-winning-the-lottery.

Chapter 10: What Matters Most

1. Jim Kouzes and Barry Posner, *A Leader's Legacy* (San Francisco: Jossey-Bass, 2006), 6.

2. John Piper, *Don't Waste Your Life* (Wheaton, IL: Crossway, 2009), 12–13; "Charles Studd," Wikipedia, https://en.wikipedia.org/wiki /Charles_Studd.

3. Matthew 25:23, NLT.

4. Luke 23:43.

5. C. S. Lewis, *Miracles: A Preliminary Study* (New York: Macmillan, 1947), 237.

6. Josh McDowell, *Evidence for the Resurrection: What It Means for Your Relationship with God* (Ventura, CA: Regal, 2009), 59.

7. See Hebrews 13:5.

8. Roy Lessin, quoted in Erik Rees, *Only You Can Be You* (Brentwood, TN: Howard, 2009), 1.

ADDITIONAL RESOURCES

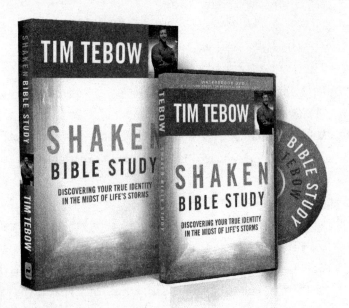

Excellent companions to *Shaken: Discovering Your True Identity in the Midst of Life's Storms*, this Bible study and DVD consist of four 9- to 12-minute sessions. These resources are an ideal package for adult and youth small groups, student athletes, and mentorship programs, as well as individual study. Join Tim as he delivers a message about what it means to fix your hope and your identity in a God who does not change.

PERFECT FOR YOUNG READERS!

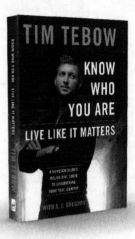

Tim Tebow encourages young people to tackle insecurity, stand out from the crowd, and develop an unshakeable identity based on God's standard—not the world's.

Tim Tebow describes the highs and the lows of his sports career and reminds young Christians that, in a world driven by "likes," the only opinion that truly matters is God's.

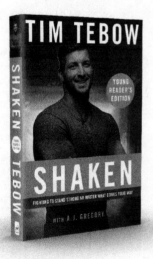

WATERBROOK

TIM TEBOW
FOUNDATION™

FAITH • HOPE • LOVE

To continue to fight for those who can't fight for themselves, a portion of proceeds from each book sold will be donated to the **Tim Tebow Foundation** to help further their mission of:

Bringing Faith, Hope and Love to those needing a brighter day in their darkest hour of need.

The foundation is currently fulfilling this mission every day by...

- Providing life-changing surgeries through the **Tebow CURE Hospital** to children of the Philippines who could not otherwise afford care.

- Creating a worldwide movement through **Night to Shine**, an unforgettable prom experience, centered on God's love, for people with special needs.

- Building **Timmy's Playrooms** in children's hospitals around the world.

- Fulfilling the dreams of children with life-threatening illnesses through the **W15H** program.

- Encouraging volunteer service to others through **Team Tebow** and **Team Tebow Kids**.

- Supporting housing, meals, medical treatment and education for orphans around the world though our **Orphan Care** program.

- Providing **Adoption Aid** financial assistance to families who are making the courageous choice to adopt a child with special needs internationally.

...simply put, Serving Children and Sharing God's Love!

To learn more about these initiatives and the continued growth of the foundation's outreach ministries, visit **www.timtebowfoundation.org**.